READY INVESTR IN REAL ESTATE

How To Create 6-Figure Passive Income That Grows While You Sleep

by

Valery Parham

READY! SET! INVEST! IN REAL ESTATE

How To Create 6-Figure Passive Income That Grows While You Sleep

By Valery Parham

Print ISBN: 979-8-9883178-0-7

LOC: On file

Design and cover art by Jeweldsign

Dedication Page

To my mother, Leslie, I want to express my gratitude for guiding me and helping me obtain my first property! I truly appreciate your wisdom and your smart real estate investing skills. I wouldn't be where I am today without your support. Thank you!

To Jeff, I also want to extend my heartfelt thanks for your assistance with my first property! Without you and my mom, I might never have embarked on my journey as a real estate investor. I appreciate your unwavering support, even during the less enjoyable aspects of homeownership, such as moving. Your willingness to help means a lot to me. Thank you!

To my maternal great-grandmother (Willie), and my maternal and paternal grandparents (Eufracia, James, Jewel and, Nathanal), thank you for investing in real estate before I was even born. I didn't realize the immense significance of your investments and the lessons you taught about the value of owning land and property as a child, but now I do! I will continue to spread your message and teachings to all who are interested in learning.

To the aspiring investors and first-time home buyers and everyone who decided to pick up this book, I want to extend a very special thank you! Your determination to learn more about real estate and your willingness to invest your time into that goal inspired me to write this book. Within these pages, I'm happy to share my knowledge and experience in the hopes that it helps you reach your wildest financial goals sooner and with greater ease!

Contents

Don't wait to buy real estate. Buy real estate and wait.
– Will Rogers

Preface

This Book Is for You If…

I was recently reminded of the story of the first person to run a mile in under 4 minutes. This feat was achieved by Roger Bannister, and since then over 1600 athletes have achieved a goal that was once thought to be impossible. This story reminds me of why I decided to write this book. You see, more and more people are finding ways to achieve their wildest dreams simply because those who have achieved a particular goal already are sharing personal stories and "how to's".

If your goals pertain to real estate, you're in the right place. This book was created to guide you through how to build your own personal real estate investing plan so that you can obtain your first property this year or possibly even this month! By sharing my personal experience and journey as a single, diverse, woman who got my start in real estate over 15 years ago, I hope to be another example showcasing that anyone can get started and make money with real estate. Many of you will even leverage the information in this book to literally make money while you live your life doing everyday things like breathing, eating, and yes, sleeping.

I am so ecstatic that you decided to read this book to learn more about real estate as you build a solid foundation on your path to real estate investing. The initiative you have taken to make this decision to invest in yourself and carve out time to build a plan shows that you are an action taker, and you are serious about growing your knowledge of real estate investment options.

Now that you have some background on what this book is all about, allow me to introduce myself and tell you a little bit more about my background and work experience. I have a bachelor's degree in civil engineering from Vanderbilt University and an MBA from Belmont University. I also am a certified

Project Management Professional and Realtor. I began my career in Engineering in 2007 and transitioned into Project Management in 2013. For many years, I have been entrusted to lead project teams on large multi-million-dollar projects, and I have also helped my real estate clients invest in millions of dollars' worth of income generating property. Now, I want to leverage my experience to help you build and achieve your goals in real estate.

I am also an avid traveler. To date I have traveled to nearly 50 countries, and in 2018 I took a 6-month trip around the world. In preparation for that trip, I wanted to create a passive income stream for myself, so I designed a layout for a home addition that I planned to rent on a short-term basis. Renting that small addition of my home consistently earned 5-figure passive income each year, and now that I rent out the entire property, I have increased my earning potential two to three times annually.

In addition to the properties I own as an individual, I co-own two additional rental units that also generate significant income each year. As a seller, I negotiated a 6-figure profit upon the sale of the first home that I ever owned. Now I want to share all my relevant experiences and what I learned along the way throughout this book.

I am a huge believer in knowing the "why". Why am I doing this? From what I've shared so far, you can see that it has taken me YEARS to accumulate the knowledge and experience that I have today. I have done things right, and I have also made mistakes. I would like you to benefit from my mistakes.

Over the years, I have observed how people define success. People believe being successful involves earning as much money as possible to buy things they want. Most people work hard to have these "things". What if you reversed that relationship and your things worked hard for you? One vehicle that makes this possible is real estate. Unfortunately, many people never get the message that their property can help them secure their retirement goals, make passive income, and grow their wealth. Many people are told that the American Dream consists of working hard so you can "own" a home. Therefore, people think they've made it when they've obtained a 30-year mortgage to live in their forever, dream home. This may be someone's American Dream, but it's not mine. My American Dream includes leveraging multiple properties and potentially multiple strategies to make money passively through real estate investments. My plan is to work to have the things that will work for me, so at some point in the near future I won't have to work anymore unless I WANT to!

As I have shared my personal story and goals, I have encountered more and more people expressing that they want to break the cycle of working to simply acquire things. They want to get into real estate, and they want income generating property of their own. Armed with my knowledge and experience, I will strive to help others achieve and surpass their goals in real estate faster and easier than my non-linear path. I want to assist people in overcoming their debilitating fears of investing and potentially failing in real estate. I will do this by helping them grow their knowledge and confidence to invest in their first properties. In doing so they can start winning in real estate like they have always had the potential to do.

Building wealth through real estate investing can lead to financial freedom. I believe that people can live their highest and best purpose using their God given talents when they aren't constrained by the need to make money through conventional methods like the 9-to-5, corporate America, job. Don't get me wrong. I wouldn't have been able to acquire the properties that I have today without the steady, increasing, regular paychecks that my 9-to-5 corporate jobs have provided. I would be remiss if I did not acknowledge the many sacrifices that come with trading time for money in the traditional job setting. Some of the things I have had to give up during my traditional career include precious time with my loved ones, my physical and mental health, and getting to be my true, authentic self all day, every day. If you have had to make similar sacrifices, imagine the impact you could have on the world if you had the basic financial security to have the <u>choice</u> to do what you wanted to each day. Would you spend more time with your family, travel more, exercise, pick up a new hobby, volunteer more, or invent something? What amazing creation or act would you give the world if you had the time and means to do so? Helping people have the financial stability to have more choices in life is a key reason why I wrote this book.

I also believe that representation matters, and I want to see more people like me represented in conversations about leveraging real estate investments to build and accumulate wealth for themselves, their families, and the generations who will come next. I believe there is enough for all of us to have what we need and desire.

I truly believe that if I can help you succeed then you can share what you learn and experience. Together, we can make a larger impact on our immediate circle of influence including our community and perhaps the entire world. That's why I am so passionate about sharing what I know with you to get this real estate, wealth-building movement started. Thank you so much for being here and being a part!

How to Get the Most from This Book

For those who have not ever purchased a home or who have a primary residence but have not invested in additional properties, the information in this book provides a step-by-step guide so you can create a personalized blueprint to your first or next real estate investment. The best part is for those who are ready to invest right now, your blueprint can be completed in 30 days or less!

If you are teachable, ready to learn, and open to new, creative ways of living to build your real estate portfolio, then this book is most definitely for you! If you are looking for a quick and easy route to real estate riches, then you may be disappointed by the approaches and tactics I share in the pages of this book. If you are comfortable doing things the tortoise's way over the hare's and you don't mind becoming wealthy at a steady pace, then the information in this book can absolutely help you! You can achieve financial stability while you do what you would be doing anyway... living life.

Now let's get into a little more about the book. As a quick overview, we will review the following topics throughout this book:

After a brief overview of *The Powerful Legacy of Real Estate!* we will begin the book with the **New Real Estate Investor Quick Start**. This section will outline quite a bit of information to build your basic knowledge of the terminology and concepts that will be used throughout the entirety of the book.

Next, we will cover key resources you need to **Build Your Real Estate Dream Team**. These resources have a lot of experience in their respective areas of expertise, so you want to lean on them to help you with your real estate investment plans. They will be there to help you avoid pitfalls, and they will provide details so you can ramp up faster than you may be able to on your own.

In **Make Dollars and Sense**, we will focus on the numbers to understand where you are today, and ultimately use this information to build to where you want to be in the near future. We will also spend time on other key considerations that you should include in your real estate investment decisions.

Niche Rental Income Options will cover some traditional and unique ways for you to get into investment properties.

Then we will discuss **Building Systems** for your investment to make things easier for you to manage.

And finally **Ready! Set! Invest!** will put everything together, so your plan is complete. With your completed plan, you'll be ready to take off and achieve your real estate investment goals.

Now let's talk a little bit about the structure. Each chapter will cover a specific topic for you to review. At the end of the chapter, a summary of the key points will be provided. Please keep in mind that some themes may be purposefully repeated to help cement the concepts in your mind. You'll have an assignment to complete at the end of each chapter as well. You can also download the Ready! Set! Invest! In Real Estate Blueprint Worksheets from my website to create a permanent copy for yourself. Please complete each assignment and include the answers you provide in your Ready! Set! Invest! in Real Estate Blueprint Worksheets. Your completed Blueprint will serve as your finalized plan that you'll have completed by the time you reach the end of this book! There will also be additional tools for you to use like the Recommended Resource Guide and the Ready! Set! Invest! in Real Estate Excel worksheets. Each will be noted in the chapter assignments so be on the lookout for those.

Now you're ready to dive into the material. Again, thank you for being here and for trusting me to be your guide on the path to your real estate investing goals! I'm so very excited for you! I truly hope you enjoy this book. May it put you on the path to financial independence so you can have the opportunity to live life more freely.

Now, let's get ready!

Let's get set!

Let's invest and start making money!

READY!

First, we will go back to the basics so you can have a solid foundation in basic real estate investment knowledge.

Introduction: The Powerful Legacy of Real Estate

One of the great privileges of my childhood life was growing up with no neighbors. At the time I didn't know not having neighbors was a privilege, so every once in a while, I would ask why we couldn't have neighbors like everyone else. To that question, my mother would always reply something to the effect of, "Why on earth would we want neighbors?! If I wanted to, I could shower outside naked in the rain, and no one would see me or care. This is freedom! This is the life!" At the time I honestly couldn't understand the appeal of showering outside naked in the rain.

I grew up in a small town on over one hundred acres of land in a simple house. I learned that the house was special though, because it was completely paid for thanks to my great grandmother who did something that most people with her background couldn't do. As a woman born in or around 1900, my great grandmother found a way to buy land, and for a time, because of her foresight and investment, my family was the largest landowner inside the city limits of my small hometown.

The house where I spent my childhood was a modest, red-brick home with a circular driveway. It had an expansive front yard with two massive pine trees planted as representations of my great grandmother's two sons. We had fruit trees (lemon, cherry, and pear), blackberry bushes, honey suckles, tulips, tiger lilies, and beautiful full hydrangeas with soft blue flowers flanking the front porch. We had a big red barn and horses. We had so much land that each year my mother planted enormous gardens with kale, greens (mustard, collards, and turnip), melons and all types of delicious fresh fruits and vegetables. One of my favorite things about the property was how vast and endless it seemed. I would often go on hikes in the backyard, and still to this day, I remember the first time I finally reached another house at the farthest edge of the property. I remember feeling like a frontiersman who had been searching for years and finally reached civilization.

I enjoyed growing up in that house and living on that land until it was time for me to go to college. And even though I enjoyed it, I didn't understand what a carefree privilege it was to grow up in that situation. Unfortunately, like most things in life, you don't miss and appreciate what you have until it's gone. The place where I grew up is one of those things that I did not fully appreciate until I no longer had it to enjoy. My family's home is only a memory in my mind now. Shortly after I went to college, the family homeland that my great grandmother acquired with the intent for us to keep and pass on through the generations was taken by the state through eminent domain. To add injury to insult, the state didn't do anything with the land. The thought of passing by where my home used to be is so painful that I have only driven past where my home used to be a handful of times in the 20 years since the land was taken away.

Thankfully, the legacy that my great grandmother created for our family did not end with that land. She planted the seeds of all the glorious benefits of owning real estate in the minds of her children, her children's children, and so on. Through the pages of this book, my great grandmother's legacy lives on and now extends to you.

That's my story, and those are some of my earliest memories of the impact of real estate in my life, but what does my story about growing up in a small town have to do with you? How can I help *YOU*? To answer that question, I want to start with an answer to a slightly different question: *Why do I believe I can help you?*

Not only do I believe I can help you, but I KNOW I can help you for the following reasons:

- *I have achieved a level of relatable success for myself.* I don't have 50 properties, and I am not making $100k per month (yet). I don't make a million dollars a year (yet). I am single, pay my own bills, work 2-3 jobs when necessary to invest and travel, and for the most part, I am frugal. At the time of writing this, I have invested in a few rentals that have generated anywhere from $10-$15k per year to $50k+ annually, and I made a substantial profit upon the sale of my very first house. These are realistic and achievable results for anyone who is getting started in real estate. That means *YOU* can absolutely use the information in this book and the personal stories I share to reach and even surpass the milestones that I have achieved to date. The key is to have a good strategy and plan, do your homework, and simply get started.

- *Not only have I achieved success for myself, I have also helped others.* I have shared my knowledge with my clients to help them develop strategies to make their investment goals come true. Depending on their unique strategy and goals, my clients have been able to consistently generate passive or semi passive income, create monthly cash flow, and experience equity growth through home value appreciation.

I helped one client get his property rented within 14 days of closing on the property. I created the Airbnb rental listing copy, and the property booked before photos were posted to the listing! The client was ecstatic to have rental income secured prior to the due date of the first mortgage payment. I advised another client on setting up her property's Airbnb listing, and she received a 3-month booking for almost $10,000 about a week later. I have even helped clients walk into equity day 1 of their purchases. One recent client purchased a property that was valued $40,000 more than the negotiated purchase price, AND the seller made additional concessions that reduced the amount of cash that she needed to close on the property. Even better, the client has been an amazing student who has paid attention and is now positioned to convert the property into a rental when she is ready to move into her next home. She went into the purchase of her first home with an investor mindset so now she's on the right path to be able to grow her portfolio!

As far as how can I help you specifically, I can help in the following ways:

- Provide basic real estate knowledge so you can build a solid foundation and understanding of real estate and real estate investing terminology, key resources to leverage, investment strategies, financing options, and other important items.

- Share pitfalls that I and others have encountered so you can avoid those roadblocks and accelerate your path to earning income and building wealth.

- Provide an easy to follow, easy to create, personalized investing blueprint that fits your goals and individual situation.

- Offer additional resources to discuss your goals and brainstorm your strategy if you get stuck or need additional assistance.

Now that you know a little more about me, and you understand how I can help you, you must decide if you are ready to commit to yourself and invest the time to continue reading this book. Through completing this book and its assignments, you'll be ready to start investing in real estate with the intention of making a return on your investment and beyond. Most importantly, by investing in real estate, you could be the seed to your family's legacy of wealth and financial freedom. That's the powerful legacy of real estate!

Section 1 New Real Estate Investor Quick Start

Chapter 1 Consider Real Estate: Why you should consider investing in real estate

In this chapter, I will cover some of the reasons why you should consider investing in and buying real estate. I mean, think about it. Why **should** you consider investing in real estate, and why **should** you spend your hard-earned money to buy property?

To those questions I would respond that everyone including you needs a place to live, and you have a couple of options. You can either rent or own or maybe consider living in your parent's basement forever for free. Of our 2 paid options (all jokes aside), you can either rent space from someone else who owns the property or you can own the property yourself.

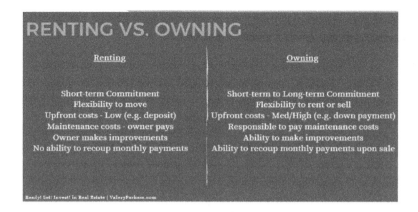

Let's start by looking at renting vs. owning. There are various reasons why you may want to rent versus why you may want to own. I will briefly touch on some high-level points for each.

Renting usually only requires a short-term commitment so renting is a good option if you need flexibility if you're not sure exactly where you are going to live for an extended period of time. Maybe you don't know because of your job or maybe it's because of other reasons. Maybe you are moving to a new area for a job, and you want to get acclimated before purchasing. In these types of scenarios, it might be a good idea for you to find something to rent for a shorter amount of time.

Along those same lines, renting gives you the flexibility to move. If you move into a place with a 12-month lease, for example, you can live in that place for 12 months to honor the terms of your lease then move to another place if you want. If something unexpected comes up, and you need to leave before the end of your lease, the penalties associated with breaking your lease might not be too steep. That type of flexibility usually makes people feel more comfortable when they are unsure of where they want to live for an extended period.

Usually as a renter, you will not have the responsibility of making improvements to the property. Property renovations, additions, and any other type of major construction activities are handled by the property owner. Similar to improvements on the property, most maintenance costs are likely going to be the responsibility of the owner as well.

Renting also usually requires a lower upfront cost. For example, renting a space might only require you to pay a security deposit whereas purchasing a property might require a down payment and closing costs.

The final consideration when thinking about renting points to one of the big drawbacks of renting which is no real ability to recoup the monthly rental payments. When you're renting, you're getting a place to live, which is great, but when it's time for you to move, that money that you paid for rent will have been spent, and there's no real way to recoup the cumulative amount that you spent every month for the duration of your rental period.

Now let's consider some points related to owning. Most people think of owning property as a very long-term commitment, and for some people that is true. For example, if you want to buy your property outright, and you have a 15-to-30-year mortgage it is going to take the full term to pay the property in full unless you use a strategy to pay the principle down faster. However, I tell overly cautious people that it doesn't have to feel so daunting. Getting a property with a mortgage doesn't have to feel like you're signing yourself up for 15, 20, or 30 years. As long as you plan on staying in the property for at least 12 to preferably 24 months then there are some benefits to being able to get that property. We'll talk about that in more detail a little bit later. If you think you're going to be in a home for at least a year or two, there are some advantages that you can take part of like capital gains tax exemptions up to certain limits depending on if you are married or single. These are some of the things to take into consideration to help you think about ownership a little bit differently. Home ownership doesn't have to be a 30-year commitment. It could be something that you're buying and just holding for a few years.

Next, when you own property, you have the flexibility to rent or sell. Let's say that you purchased a property, and let's say you have only had it for a few years. You decide that you need to or want to move for whatever reason. At that point, depending on how the market is performing, you could either sell or rent your property. If you sell you will potentially make a profit. If you need or want to hold the property you can consider renting. Hopefully, the realization that home ownership comes with some elements of flexibility will lift the cloud of pressure and thinking "oh my goodness one day I might be in a bind and need to sell but the market isn't favorable right now." If that situation arises or even if the market is great, you have options.

You as the owner have the flexibility to make improvements to your property, and making improvements could increase the value of the property. You're putting money into the property, but you're potentially going to be able to get that value on the back end when it's time for you to sell the property. That is another benefit of being an owner of a property.

Now, the upfront cost associated with purchasing a property could be considerable. You will probably need a down payment, and there will be closing costs for obtaining a loan. There may be certain things that need to be enhanced at the property so you will want to consider that when you're thinking about buying something. In the same breath, I also want to mention that it doesn't have to be so challenging, and the upfront costs might not be an astronomical amount. There are different down payment options, and I will cover this topic in a later chapter. I will walk through speaking with your lender about those different down payment options because that may be a way for you to get your foot into the property ownership door. If the down payment is something that seems like a huge hurdle for you, there may be ways to acquire your property without having to make such a large down payment.

As the owner, you will be responsible for paying maintenance costs, but keep in mind you want to keep your property maintained because it is an investment that you're making for yourself. If you purchase a car, for example, you take it to get serviced, you buy new tires, you wash the car and clean the car's interior, you change the oil, and other tasks to maintain the car's performance. You'll want to do the same thing for the property that you are investing in. You will want to refresh the paint, do small repairs, keep it clean, maintain the landscaping, and generally keep the property in good condition. Depending on your strategy, it's either something that you're buying so that you can live in it and enjoy it for as long as you like or it's something that you are buying to get a return on your investment. You're going to want to make sure that just like the car analogy, your house is a well-oiled machine.

Finally, when you think about owning a property, (we will go through an example a little bit later) you will have the ability to recoup some of those monthly payments that you're making upon the sale. I say SOME, but you may be able to recoup all of the monthly payments that you make. You may be able to profit and basically live for free and even make money back. Absolutely consider this when you're thinking about renting vs. owning.

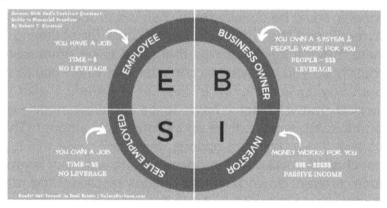

Before getting into your potential starting points, I wanted to introduce you to some concepts from the book "Rich Dad's Cash Flow Quadrant" by Robert Kiyosaki. From a high level, what I want to introduce right now is the left-hand side of this diagram and the contrast to the right-hand side.

On the left-hand side, you have the E and S quadrants. These stand for the Employee quadrant and the Self-employed or small business owner. There are some benefits to being in either of these two quadrants, however, when you are in these quadrants, you must work to make money. If you stop working, your money stops.

In contrast, when you move to the B or I quadrants on the right-hand side of the diagram, as either a big business owner or an investor, you can leverage other people's time and other people's money to make money.

Being able to make money using other people's time and money, frees you up to do more of the things you want to do in life while still generating income. Having more time freedom while making money independently of your direct efforts is a win-win situation, and investing in real estate is one vehicle that enables you to make money leveraging other people's time and money.

I think the Cash Flow Quadrant is a great illustration and introduction into why having systems to create passive income is so important. With that in mind, I wanted to introduce you to Kiyosaki's book if you haven't read it already. If you have read it before, now may be a good time to re-read this book and continue to learn and re-wire your thinking as you grow in your journey as an investor.

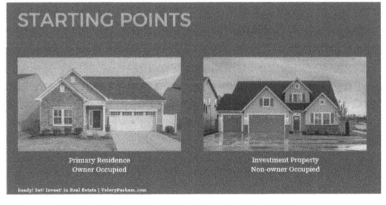

I have hinted a little bit already that there are some

different starting points for those who haven't already amassed several properties. If you're reading this book, I'm assuming that currently you do not own a property or maybe you only own your primary residence. I will go through two scenarios. You may be acquiring a primary residence where you as the owner are going to be occupying that residence. That's one place that you can start. If you already own your primary residence, you may be trying to figure out how to find and acquire an investment property. That investment is for something that you own for the purpose of having guests and renters who pay you money to live in the property. I will focus on these two starting points throughout the remainder of this book.

PRIMARY RESIDENCE

REAL ESTATE PROPERTY PURCHASED FOR THE PURPOSE OF PRIMARY LIVING

A principal residence is the primary location that a person inhabits. It is also referred to as a primary residence or main residence. It does not matter whether it is a house, apartment, trailer, or boat, as long as it is where an individual, couple, or family household lives most of the time.

- Investopedia

Ready! Set! Invest! in Real Estate ValeryParham.com

I want to make sure that everybody is starting on the same level playing field. Let's start by covering what a primary residence is. A primary residence is the primary location that a person inhabits. This is also referred to as a principal residence or main residence. It doesn't matter whether it's a house, apartment, trailer, or boat as long as it's where an individual, couple, or family intend to live most of the time. The purpose of your primary residence is where you're going to be living most of the time.

THE BENEFITS OF A PRIMARY RESIDENCE

WHY IT'S A GREAT INVESTMENT OPTION

Flexibility   Appreciation   Diversification   Tax Benefits

Let's focus on the benefits of a primary residence. When thinking of owning a primary residence, flexibility is a benefit that quickly comes to mind. When it's time for you to move, you have the flexibility to either sell the house OR rent the house. This flexibility can be combined with other house hacking strategies that will be outlined in later chapters.

You're also going to get an opportunity for your property to increase in value through appreciation. Depending on the market and other factors, your house may appreciate in value while you're living there. While you're doing your thing and living life, major changes in your home's area or other properties being enhanced around you can change the marketability of your property. If new industry comes into your area, your home value may increase even more. While you're paying down your mortgage, you're going to start to build and accumulate additional equity in your home. This ability for your home to appreciate in several ways gives you a great opportunity to potentially make money while you're virtually doing nothing except what you were going to be doing anyway.

Another great thing about having a primary residence is diversification. Asset diversification is basically the concept of not putting all of your eggs in one basket. You may have a savings account, you may have a 401k, you may have stock options through your company or some other form of investing that you're doing, but you may also have a primary residence.

Your primary residence has the potential to grow in value while you are simply living and breathing there. Without owning a primary residence, you are potentially missing out of that diversification avenue. You should strongly consider owning a primary residence for this particular benefit: diversification of your assets.

Finally, there are the tax benefits. This is a topic you will want to talk about with a tax professional because there are many benefits associated with having a primary residence. Make sure you ask your tax professional about the beauty of the Capital Gains Tax exemption.

OWNERSHIP STORY

1st Home
- Committed to living in home at least 2 years
- Enjoyed the home for years prior to selling
- Made improvements over time
- Upfront costs - 0% down payment w/ initial improvements
- Minimal maintenance costs outside of lawncare
- Recouped the cost of living in the home for many years w/ the added benefit of capital gains tax exemption

Let's now get into a quick story. I want to share how I started my journey so pictured here is my first property ever. I always give my mother credit for helping me find this diamond in the rough. I know you may look at the picture, and you may not see a diamond, but this house really started it all for me.

I acquired this property in 2007, and my goal at the time was to live in the home for at least 2 years to take advantage of that capital gains tax exemption benefits I mentioned earlier. At the time I was fresh out of college, and my mother came to Nashville to help me look for a home. We were driving one day, and we came across this house. As we were approaching the home, she said "hey, stop at that property. There are papers in the window." I said, "What does that mean?" She said, "It's winterized," and I said, "What does *that* mean," and she said, "It's a foreclosure, please just pull over and let's take a look at it!" I saw it, and it had this rickety handrailing and the landscaping clearly is not up to par as you can see in the photo. I wish I still had some pictures of the inside of what it originally looked like when we were in the process of buying it. There was this really awful burnt orange colored paint on the walls, and it wasn't even a smooth finish of paint. It also had old, dirty carpet that was not very nice. It was not something that was visually appealing for me as my first home. I definitely wanted to have something that was much better, much nicer, and much, much bigger.

My mother said, "This will not be your forever home. This is just your starter home. Let's get you started. It's something that you can afford so consider it." The good news about this story is I enjoyed this home for many, many years prior to selling.

I did make improvements over time. As you can see there weren't even basic things like shutters on the house. I made changes over time that really enhanced the character of the house. I redid the landscaping, redid the floors, then redid the paint on the inside. The small things over time really helped. The upfront costs were very minimal. To begin with, we were able to get a zero down payment option and then we just had to come together to make some of the initial improvements. I lived in this house for nine years, way longer than the two years that I had originally planned.

This 1950s home required very minimal maintenance and for the most part, all I had to do was hire someone to do the yard work. After I got settled in, I enjoyed this house so much that I didn't want to move. When I finally sold the property, my profits were more than my combined 9 years of mortgage payments. I realized by buying instead of renting, I had basically paid myself to live in the home. We will go through that example next.

THE NUMBERS

- Prior to my 1st home, I rented.
- Rent = $950 / month
- Mortgage on my 1st home = $650 / month

Rent for 9 years = $950 x 12 months x 9 years
Rent for 9 years = $102,600

Mortage for 9 years = $650 x 12 months x 9 years
Mortage for 9 years = $70,200

Here is the landscape of my living situation at the time. I was living with a friend from college in a condo that her parents owned, and I paid $950 per month to live with her in the two-bedroom condo. When I moved into my first property, my mortgage was around $650 per month. If I had stayed in a situation where I was renting from someone else and paying $950 per month, I would have spent over $100,000.

THE NUMBERS

- I saved $32,400 by owning compared to renting over the same period of time.
- I also made a little over $100,000 when I sold my first home
- Less what my mortgage cost over 9 years, I made $29,800 to live in the home.

Not only did I essentially live for free, I made money from simply living in the home!

This is the power of property value appreciation.

By buying I reduced my housing costs to around $70,000 dollars over those 9 years. This was a savings of over $30,000, and when I sold the property, I made a little over $100,000 in profit so I like to think of it as essentially paying myself almost $30,000 to live in that house. This is the power of property value appreciation and home ownership.

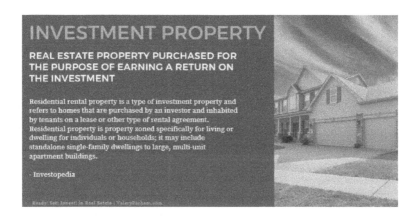

Now that we've gone through that example of making money from an owner-occupied primary residence, let's review investment property. Investment property is real estate that's purchased for the purpose of earning a return on your investment. Now, I'm going to cover residential rental property specifically. This is a type of investment property that refers to homes that are purchased by an investor. The property is inhabited by tenants who have a lease or some other type of rental agreement with you. Residential property is property that's zoned specifically for living or dwelling for individuals or households. It may include stand-alone single-family dwellings to large multi-unit apartment buildings. That's just a quick high-level explanation of the difference between a primary residence and an investment property. When you're thinking about an investment property you know that the purpose from the start is to earn a return on your investment.

What are some benefits of rental property? When we take a quick look at the benefits of rental property, there are some things that mirror the benefits of your primary residence. In addition to those there are two major benefits that I want to call out. The first one is passive income. When you have an investment property, depending on how you set it up, you have the ability to truly wake up and just see money in the bank. There are things that you're going to have to do to set the property up, like acquire it and get it ready for renting. Once you get it set up you will virtually be making money as you sleep while somebody else is living there. As long as everything is running smoothly, there's nothing more for you to do. By owning a quality property that you keep well maintained, with good systems in place, you can truly make passive income.

Speaking of passive income, one of the other things here that I've called out is that other people pay. Other people are using their paycheck to pay for your investment and that is something that is truly amazing about real estate investment property. It's awesome because you are providing great space for people that they need, want, like, and enjoy. All the while they're helping you pay for your asset while that asset is likely appreciating in value. That is the double multiplier effect that I love about rental properties. The other thing to quickly mention is that when you think about tax benefits there are some additional tax benefits of owning rental property as well. I am not a certified public accountant (CPA), but you should definitely consider getting with a tax professional to learn more about those tax benefits. For example, I make sure to keep track of all of the expense that are necessary to maintain and operate my rental property. I can leverage many of those expenses as tax write offs because it's the cost of doing business when you are providing space to renters.

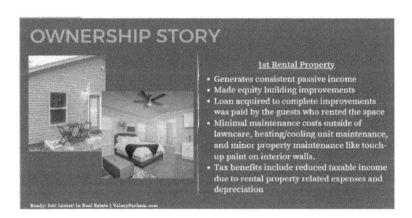

Now let's take a quick look at how I got into my first rental property. During the intro, I mentioned that I planned a 6-month trip around the world. While I was gone on the trip, I wasn't going to have a job so I wasn't going to be making money. I thought to myself wouldn't it be nice if I had an opportunity to still have some income coming in while I'm traveling. I had also wanted to have a rental property for many years, so I added some square footage to my home to be able to have my first rental property.

The great thing about this rental property is that once it was set up, it generated consistent, passive income. I had a property management company manage this for me while I was away and was not involved at all. I was literally on the other side of the world and received money in my bank account monthly.

The additional square footage that I added to my primary residence helped me to build some additional equity in the home as well. I did use a loan to complete the improvements, so I leveraged someone else's money to add this additional square footage. The money that my guests paid to stay in the space helped to pay that loan every month. There was minimal maintenance cost outside of lawn care, heating and cooling unit maintenance, and minor things like touch up paint on the interior walls. As touched on earlier, there were some good tax benefits that I was able to leverage to reduce my taxable income including things like relevant expenses and depreciation.

COMPOUNDING PROFITS IN PROPERTY

RENTAL INCOME
From other people's paychecks (OPP).

PASSIVE INCOME / SEMI-PASSIVE INCOME
Set it up to make money in your sleep.

INCOME FROM FUTURE RESALE
when you are ready to sell, make an additional income if the sales price is greater than what is owed on the property.

To tie all of these things together, I want to touch on compounding profits in property. One of the first key items that I've touched on is rental income that you're getting from other people's paychecks. Other people are paying for your asset, which is amazing. You're going to get passive or semi-passive income. Depending on how you setup your systems, you can seriously make money in your sleep. I know people say that. I know you may not believe it. I know it sounds wild, but there will be days that you literally wake up and haven't done anything else to the property and you will get a paycheck. Depending on how the market's going, how long you've held the asset, the location, and other factors, you could potentially make income from the future sale of the property as well. Think about it. You're making a recurring income with little or no additional effort once your system is set up. When you're ready to sell your property, you're going to make even more money if the sale price is greater than what is owed on the property. All of these are great and wonderful benefits owning real estate.

Chapter 1 Activities

Review the chapter questions and enter the answers in the lesson's worksheet in the Ready! Set! Invest! In Real Estate Blueprint located at the end of this book.

- Do you currently rent or own?

- Of the benefits outlined during this chapter, which ownership benefits appeal to you most?

- Why are you most interested in those benefits?

Chapter 2 Your "Foundation" & Your "Why": Setting your motivational "Foundation"& Defining your "Why"

In this chapter, I want to discuss foundation, and not the foundation of a house. Instead let's talk about your motivational foundation and defining your *why*. I stated earlier in the book that knowing your why is extremely important, so we will cover your why in this chapter. Let's get to it!

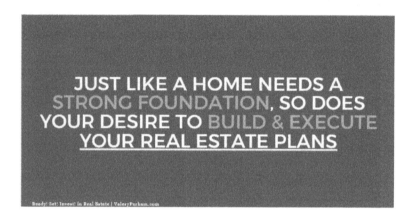

JUST LIKE A HOME NEEDS A
STRONG FOUNDATION, SO DOES
YOUR DESIRE TO BUILD & EXECUTE
YOUR REAL ESTATE PLANS

Ready! Set! Invest! in Real Estate | ValeryParham.com

Just like a home needs a strong foundation, so does your desire to build and execute your real estate goals and plans. Instead of thinking about simply buying a first or second property, treat the transaction as though you were building a business. If you think about it that way, you definitely have to have a strong conviction and understanding of why you are getting into real estate. I covered some of the pros and cons of getting into real estate earlier in the book. For example, you have to spend money to make money in real estate. Having a strong, unbreakable connection to your "why" will help you along your path. You are literally investing time, money, and effort into building something for yourself, your family, and the long-term. That's why you must have a strong foundation.

Another perspective is this: "**In investing, what is comfortable is rarely profitable**." Think about that statement. To be successful we must take a moment to get out of our comfort zone. Let's talk about that.

Let's be open. Let's be comfortable with being uncomfortable. As we build a plan to create a wildly profitable venture that builds and compounds over time we have to stretch beyond our norm. Stretching beyond your comfort zone will allow you to expand your current opportunities to create infinite possibilities in your life. This topic gets me so excited because it can literally change your life! I hope it gets you excited as well.

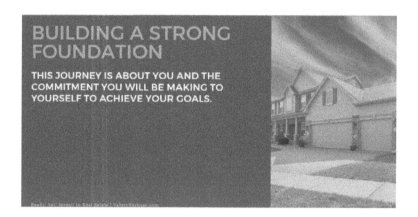

As I continue the discussion about building a strong foundation, keep in mind that this particular journey is all about you. It's all about you and the commitment that you are making to yourself to achieve your goals. Things won't always be easy. Life is definitely going to throw curveballs at you. There will be moments when you don't feel like there are enough hours in the day to focus on what you want to accomplish. When those days come, say these affirmations as a reminder of the commitment that you've made to see your ideas and goals through to completion. It is extremely important that we kick things off with the right mindset and intentions so that you are set up for success and have an unbreakable foundation. Let's look at the affirmations for your goal achievement.

Remember, I talked about this a moment ago. It's not always going to be easy. You're going to have to dig deep. When things get hard, when things are challenging, I want these affirmations to be something that you can easily access. These affirmations are true! They are also true about you.

Number one: I can achieve anything with the right mindset, will power, and desire. There is nothing that you can't achieve. The important part for you to take away is you absolutely can do anything that you put your mind to if you are willing to work at it and you have a strong desire to see it through to completion.

As you progress, there will be different activities that you must do to get into the real-estate world. With that in mind I want you to think about affirmation **number two**: I will only focus on goals that are aligned with my "why". There will be things that come up. There will be distractions. You'll really have to pull yourself away and focus on the goals that will empower you and get you where you want to go. These goals should be strongly aligned with your "why".

Number three: I will set clear, focused goals and I will work on one goal at a time one day at a time. We have to make our intentions very clear so I will talk about goal setting and how to make your goals specific later in the book. When you're dealing with a big, audacious goal, think of your goal like an elephant and try to consume it one bite at a time. When you think to yourself that you have to do everything all at once, it's extremely difficult to achieve any goal, let alone a big goal. With that in mind, I've designed this book so that you have small assignments. By the end of this book, those small assignments will collectively come together and form your complete plan. Always try to focus on the daily or weekly assignment, and together, we will make progress toward your goal.

Number four: I will take action mindfully so that I am prioritizing actions that move me towards completing my goals. This is imperative because after you have set your goals, you must take action and that action has to be with a purpose. Like I mentioned earlier, there will be a multitude of inconveniences thrown at you on a regular basis so prioritizing those actions is going to be vital.

Number five: Failure is okay as long as I'm unwilling to accept defeat. Know that failure can be leveraged as a learning opportunity so that you can grow and avoid a pitfall the next time. Do not be afraid of failure. Just make sure to pick yourself up and carry on.

Number six: If I fail, I am not a failure! You are never a failure. You will not fail, but if ever you have a moment when you feel like you have failed at something, just remember that *you* are not a failure.

Number seven: I will learn through failure, and I will try again and again until I achieve my goal. In the book, Think and Grow Rich, there is a story about gentleman who learned a valuable lesson. He was only 3 feet from his goal, but he stopped before reaching his goal. Below is a link to a video to this story if you want to learn more. It's worth watching because it's a great illustration of not only persistence but also how you can learn from your quote unquote "failures."

Number eight: I know failure is temporary because I choose to move past failure quickly. Never wallow in anything that feels like failure. Leverage your support system, leverage our community and those around you who want to see you succeed. Pick yourself up, learn from the experience, and continue to go forward.

This next one is so very important to me. I hope it resonates with you as well. **Number 9:** I will not allow fear to keep me from starting or moving forward. In life, there is literally a first time for everything we've done or accomplished. Imagine taking your first steps as a child and literally putting one foot in front of the other for the first time or applying to and getting your first job. Those "first time" situations can be extremely scary. However, if you will just commit to yourself that you will start, you can achieve anything you want in life! No matter what, put one foot in front of the other just as you did when you were a child and continue to move forward.

And **number 10**: I can, and I will! You absolutely will be able to achieve any goal that you set for yourself, and I'm here to help you every step of the way.

To drive home the point just a little more, remember, "the only thing worse than starting something and failing, is not starting something." Really let that sink in! Anytime you think about a tough goal that intimidates you, remember this point and just take one small step, then another and another until you reach your goal.

Let's now turn our focus to Why. I have been mentioning this from the beginning. Why start? Why do anything? Why do you want to get into real estate? Understanding your why and personal reasons for doing the things you set out to do is so paramount because of everything we talked about earlier. When challenges come your way, when work is frustrating you, when family life is challenging, when your savings account takes a hit, you must understand your why.

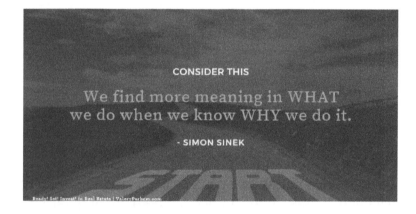

"We find more meaning in what we do when we know why we do it." Knowing your why is going to help you understand and connect with your purpose for attacking the goals you've set in real estate. Understanding and anchoring to your personal why will help motivate you to continue when everything's not going exactly how you planned. With that in mind, remember that this chapter is all about setting intentions. It's all about being focused on you and what you're trying to accomplish and understanding why you are trying to accomplish. Pay close attention to this chapter of the book. It will help you stay rooted in your reasons to get into real estate while you are building your plan. Again, I'll leave you with this thought as you go into the chapter assignment: "We find more meaning in what we do when we know why we do it."

Chapter 2 Activities

Review the chapter questions and enter the answers in the lesson's worksheet in the Ready! Set! Invest! In Real Estate Blueprint.

- Print the Goal Achievement Affirmations list and place it somewhere where you will see it each day. Read the affirmations silently or out loud each day to encourage you throughout your real estate achievement journey.

- Spend at least 30 focused minutes in a quiet space to write down your why in the Ready! Set! Invest! In Real Estate Blueprint.

Chapter 3 Creative Inspiration: Inspiration from someone leveraging real estate to reach her financial goals.

Let's dive into some creative inspiration to get your mind thinking about the possibilities.

The example that I will cover in this chapter is about someone leveraging real estate to reach her financial goals. Her name is Sylvia Hall.

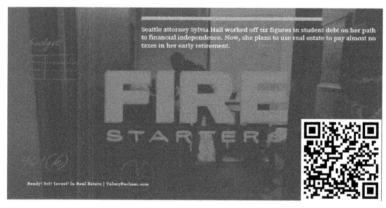

I first learned about Sylvia's story when a friend shared a Fire Starters video about the Seattle-based attorney. In the video, Sylvia shares insights about her path to FIRE. You can see her video if you use the QR Code in the corner of the above graphic.

For those who don't know, FIRE or F-I-R-E stands for financial, independence, retire early. I know FIRE is not for everyone, but even if FIRE is not your cup of tea or something that you are interested in, I do want you to take note of some key takeaways from Sylvia's story. Let's get into the details!

#1 Know Where Your Money Goes

BUDGET

Sylvia's monthly budget (2009)

401(k)*:	$1,375	* automatic deductions
Roth IRA*:	$417	
Student loans*:	$2,371	
Rent*:	$1,000	
Renters insurance*:	$10	
Car insurance*:	$77	
Gasoline:	$15	
Groceries:	$60	
Discretionary spending:	$250	Total: $5,575

One of the first key things that I took away from the video is that Sylvia is very intentional about understanding where her money goes. She has a budget, and in that budget, she keeps track of what she is spending so that she understands if all her dollars are contributing to her ultimate why which is being able to achieve Financial Independence. Like Sylvia, we also need to understand our budget to see if everything we have in our budget aligns with the things that bring us value. Now, this is not the moment where I tell you that you need to be super restrictive in your spending, but I do think understanding your budget and where your money is currently going is important especially when you're thinking about investing in real estate. Sylvia's example further illustrates that you don't have to make an extremely high income to invest in real estate. You do however, have to know where you are spending your money. When you know where your money is currently going, you can evaluate different scenarios to really build out a plan for where you want your money to go in the future. You will also be able to evaluate different options for acquiring your real estate investments. That is why key take away #1 from the video is to know where your money goes.

#2 Understand Your Net Worth

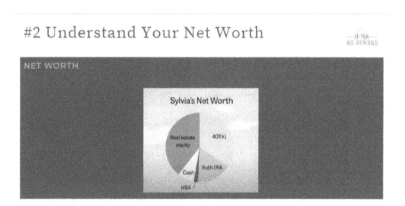

Key take away #2 is to understand your net worth. Your net worth is not something that you have to look at every single day, but it is important. I talked about diversification earlier in the book. During the Fire Starter video, Sylvia talked about her net worth and showed the breakdown of her assets. I thought it was very interesting that a large part of her net worth comes from her real estate equity.

From my experience working with clients, net worth is a topic that can bring some anxiety and hesitation. You may have feelings of resistance when it is time to calculate your net worth. Remember it's okay to be uncomfortable during this process and push forward to do the assignment. Knowing your starting point and establishing your net worth baseline will be very helpful as you make strides on your investment journey.

In the Fire Starters video, Sylvia mentioned a point when she was at negative net worth and how excited she was to get back to a net worth of ZERO. This should be relatable for most people especially those who accumulated high amounts of student loan debt before getting your first job. It does not matter if you are in the negative, if you were at breakeven, or if you have enough to retire already. The point is to simply know where you stand. I encourage everyone reading this book to take a moment and understand what their current net worth is. This will help you create a baseline for where you are today, and also give you an opportunity to think about where you want to be in the future.

#3 Identify Tax Benefits & Deductions

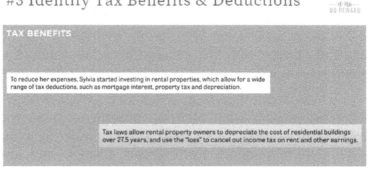

Key take away #3 covers identifying tax benefits and deductions. In this example, Sylvia focused on investing in rental properties which helped her leverage tax deductions. She used tax deductions like mortgage interest, property tax, and depreciation to her benefit to reduce her taxable income. For those of you who do not have any type of real estate already, these benefits are possible reasons why it might be time for you to go ahead and get started in real estate.

One of the other benefits mentioned detailed how Sylvia leverages depreciation to reduce her taxable income. There are so many tax benefits associated with real estate, and they change all the time. I highly recommend speaking with a tax professional about the various ways you can take advantage of the many benefits that come with owning property.

#4 Start Somewhere Then Grow

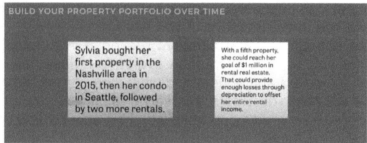

BUILD YOUR PROPERTY PORTFOLIO OVER TIME

Sylvia bought her first property in the Nashville area in 2015, then her condo in Seattle, followed by two more rentals.

With a fifth property, she could reach her goal of $1 million in rental real estate. That could provide enough losses through depreciation to offset her entire rental income.

This fourth key take away is something we discussed in an earlier chapter which is to simply start somewhere. We do this throughout our lives with nearly everything, but for some reason at some point, we get into a mindset where we want everything immediately. Life usually doesn't work like that.

Think about it. We start in kindergarten, we go through elementary school, high school, college, and so forth. Our educational journeys start with simple, building blocks. We create our foundation from those blocks and grow our knowledge from there. When you apply that analogy to real estate, you realize that a multi-unit apartment building may ot be your starting point. You can, however, absolutely start with a primary residence. You could also start with your first one-to-four-unit rental property. Get some basic knowledge on how investing in real estate works. Dip your toe in the water and try ownership for yourself. Build those muscles first to become more comfortable. THEN you can start to acquire more properties or maybe you can start to amass bigger properties or maybe you get properties that are in another location.

There are so many options if you'll just start somewhere.

In Sylvia's video, it's noted that her first property was in the Nashville area. After her first property, she purchased a condo in Seattle and acquired two more rentals. By the time she was able to get her fifth property, she reached her goal of having $1 million dollars in real estate. Building a real estate portfolio can take a little bit of time. It's not a get-rich-quick scheme, but you can absolutely do it! Depending on the local market, some people are seeing investments they made years ago explode! The lesson here is you just have to start somewhere and then incrementally build. Take care of your investment, and your investment will take care of you.

#5 Leverage Financing

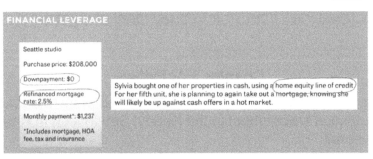

Number 5: Personally, I think this is one of the most incredible things about real estate: Financial leverage. There are so many options to be able to leverage financing so that you can hold on to more of your liquid money but still have the benefits of owning property. There aren't many assets that you can buy leveraging someone else's money that are going to potentially appreciate for you. I think that is so cool, so amazing, and so wonderful! That's why I tell so many people that if they are interested in and considering real estate, financing is something that they should learn more about and take advantage of. There are also special programs to help you reach your goals regardless of your financial situation.

In Sylvia's example, she was able to acquire her studio

with 0% down, and she was able to obtain a mortgage at a very, very low rate: 2.5%. On top of all that, she used another perk of real estate. As her property grew in equity, she leveraged the equity to purchase another asset to add to her portfolio. In this example, Sylvia purchased one of her properties in cash by using a home equity line of credit. From this video, you can see how over time Sylvia has used many of the benefits of owning real estate over and over to acquire more properties. She grew her property portfolio using a repeatable system, and you can too!

I hope this summary of Sylvia's inspirational video really sparked your interests and got your creative juices flowing. Like I said earlier in this chapter, FIRE is for everyone, and it may not be for you, but some of the key takeaways from her experience are relevant for everyone and can work for you. That's why your assignment for this chapter is to consider these key takeaways from your own personal perspective.

Chapter 3 Activities

Review the chapter questions and enter the answers in the lesson's worksheet in the Ready! Set! Invest! In Real Estate Blueprint.

- Consider what you read in this chapter about Sylvia. What were some interesting takeaways you learned? Note: It could be one of the 5 noted in the chapter or other takeaways that resonated with you.

- What are some creative ways Sylvia is leveraging her real estate? Are there any you would consider for your real estate journey?

- Write down tax benefits you would receive or have received as a property owner and note additional tax benefits you would receive as a rental property owner.

Chapter 4 Get Ready! Stay Ready!: Understand your finances; stay ready so you don't have to get ready

This chapter is all about getting ready and staying ready. I will continue to build on some of the concepts that I mentioned in the previous chapter so you can apply them to your unique situation. In chapter 3, I was prepping you with the concepts by walking through the creative example to get you thinking about what's possible. In this chapter, you are going to take those concepts and actually work through your situation so you can get ready and stay ready.

The whole point of this chapter is all about understanding your finances. It's critically important to make sure that when the right opportunity presents itself, you are already ready so that you don't have to get ready. This is crucial because when real estate markets are hot, properties go very, very quickly.

Buyers have to be ready, and they have to stay ready if they want to acquire the property they want as soon as it hits the market. In real estate, time is of the essence. This means that you could miss an opportunity to another buyer if you are not prepared to make a decision swiftly. Let's make sure that you stay ready so when the right opportunity presents itself you are prepared and ready to go, and you can strike while the iron is hot. Okay, I know you've got it so let's get ready and stay ready!

This chapter will be short because you've been taking in a lot of information. This chapter's homework is going to be a little more involved, so you'll need a good amount of focused time to complete the assignment. In the previous chapter, the first key takeaway that I mentioned as I reviewed Sylvia's story was knowing where your money goes. Just like Sylvia has a budget, you are going to work through what your budget looks like.

#1 Know Where Your Money Goes

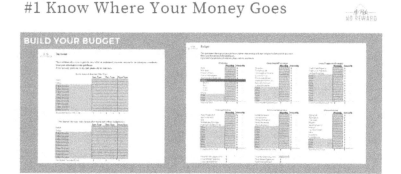

To help with this activity, I have some Ready! Set! Invest! in Real Estate Excel worksheets. There is a budget template that is already set up for you to enter your specific information to better understand your current financials. This is important so you can understand if there are some areas of your spending where you may want to cut back a little bit as you prepare to invest in real estate. For example, if you want to build a reserve for the property you want to acquire, you would want to make sure that you have a budget and you understand where your money is currently going.

#2 Understand Your Net Worth

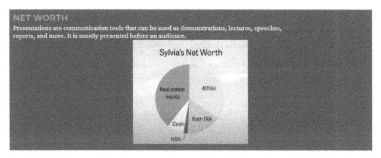

Key takeaway number 2 was understanding your net worth. This is something that I haven't always done. I've kept a budget for an extremely long time. I can go back at least 10 years with my budget information that I've updated over the years, but I have not kept up with my net worth until recently. For many people, I think tracking net worth is simply not top of mind. Others, I believe, avoid tracking their net worth because they are a little anxious about what they think they're going to find when they check it.

#2 Understand Your Net Worth

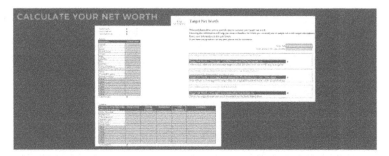

I don't want anybody in this course to be intimidated by this chapter. The purpose of these activities is all about understanding where you are today. This goes back to, yet again, what we discussed earlier in the book regarding being comfortable with being a little uncomfortable. As you continue through this book and build on previous lessons, if there's an activity that feels a little uncomfortable, I want you to push through that feeling to complete the activity. If you are feeling uneasy about calculating your net worth, do it anyway. Fill out the net worth portions of your Excel worksheet. It will be a valuable tool as you envision how to leverage real estate to create your net worth over the years.

The last thing that I want to cover in this lesson is what you want your starting point to be. Are you currently renting or staying with friends or family? If you have not purchased a primary residence and that is something you would like to do as a starting point, then make note of that starting point in the chapter assignment. If you already have a primary residence, then maybe getting an investment property is your next step. Keep those two options in mind when selecting your starting point.

As promised, this chapter is quick and to the point so you can have time to work on the assignment.

Chapter 4 Activities

Review the chapter questions and enter the answers in the lesson's worksheet in the Ready! Set! Invest! In Real Estate Blueprint.

- Know Where Your Money Goes – Fill out the income and budget spreadsheets provided.

- Understand Your Net Worth – Fill out the Net Worth and Target Net Worth spreadsheets provided. Note: If your net worth is negative, zero, or off target, try not to be intimidated, frustrated, or feel down. Remember the goal at this point is to understand your starting point and where you are now.

- Start Somewhere Then Grow – List your current starting point. Where would you like to start (primary residence or investment property)? When is your goal to invest (e.g. ASAP, 1-3 months, 3-6 months, 6-12 months, more than 12 months)?

Section 2 Build your real estate dream team

Chapter 5 Realtor & Lenders: Benefits of having a Realtor & a Lender on your real estate Dream Team.

In this chapter, you will learn about the best resources to have on your team as you dive deeper into your real estate plan. Ready to go? I sure hope so. Let's jump into it.

In chapter 6, we'll focus on two key resources that you'll want to have on your team, regardless of whether you're purchasing your first home or your fifth investment property. Those two resources are Realtors and lenders.

REALTORS

WHY YOU NEED ONE ON THE DREAM TEAM

1. ETHICAL TREATMENT
2. AN EXPERT GUIDE
3. OBJECTIVE INFORMATION AND OPINIONS
4. EXPANDED SEARCH POWER
5. NEGOTIATION KNOWLEDGE
6. UP-TO-DATE EXPERIENCE
7. YOUR ROCK DURING EMOTIONAL MOMENTS

Let's start with realtors. You should absolutely have a realtor on your real estate dream team. Licensed real estate agents who are also Realtors bring so many benefits to the table. For starters, licensed agents have a high degree of responsibility when acting on behalf of their clients. Agents by law must act in a manner that places their clients' interests above all others' interests, including the agent's own self-interests. They are also required to keep you informed of all facts and any other information that could impact you or your transaction.

Being a realtor kicks these high standards even higher. Realtors understand that the best and highest use of the land and the widest distribution of land ownership facilitates the interests of the nation and all of its citizens. To become a member of the National Association of Realtors (NAR), aspiring

Realtors must study and adhere to the NAR's Code of Ethics and Standards of Practice. As noted in the Code's preamble, Realtors have a duty to clients, customers, the public, and each other to continuously strive to become and remain informed on issues affecting real estate. As knowledgeable professionals, they willingly share the fruits of their experience and study with others. They identify and take steps through enforcement of the Code of Ethics and by assisting appropriate regulatory bodies to eliminate practices which may damage the public or which might discredit or bring dishonor to the real estate profession. As you consider your next real estate investment, know that a realtor's main obligation is to you and your real estate related needs. They hold professionalism and the ethical treatment of you and all parties involved to the highest regard.

Realtors are also experts who can guide you through the twists and turns of real estate transactions. Each transaction is unique, and they usually require several contract documents, disclosures, back and forth communications, and lots of coordination to make it from the initial offer to the closing table. It's a realtor's job to navigate these waters on a regular basis, so they are expertly versed in the processes and jargon associated with real estate transactions. Realtors can also supply you with objective information and opinions. They leverage their knowledge of the areas in which they work, along with data sources and tools to provide you with information regarding zoning, proposed area developments and more. They keep a pulse on market trends and can also provide you with an objective viewpoint on a property as it relates to your goals and needs. Since no two properties are 100% alike, real estate can evoke a certain amount of subjectivity, especially for new investors. Realtors can point you to objective information to help you during the decision-making process. This is another key benefit of having a Realtor on your Real Estate Dream Team.

Today there are websites and apps where you can search for listed properties. While these tools are great starting points to use, you may be missing out on available properties that fit your search criteria. Realtors can also help in this area because they are savvy. They can help you find properties that are listed on sites that you might not be familiar with, properties that are coming soon, or even properties that haven't been listed yet. When it comes to real estate transactions and the contract terms associated with the deal, there are many aspects that are open for negotiation. Realtors have negotiating knowledge, and they will use that knowledge to look at every angle of the deal for your benefit. For example, making sure that you have enough time to complete due diligence activities like inspections before you are bound to complete a purchase is a key aspect of property negotiations. Having a realtor assist you with items like this during the negotiation process can provide much peace of mind for a new investor. The landscape of real estate and buying and selling property is always changing and evolving. Laws and regulations change. Market sentiment can shift and favor sellers or buyers. Since buying and selling property isn't something that you do on a regular basis, it helps to have a realtor assist you with the process. They have up to date experience with the changes through dealing with real estate transactions on a consistent basis.

Lastly, Realtors are there for you through the emotional moments of the home buying process. The reality is purchasing property can be a very emotionally taxing process. I personally have experienced this as someone who has been through the process a few times myself. Being out bid on a property that you had your heart set on is a disappointing situation that could occur when you are making offers on properties. Having your offer accepted only to walk away from a deal during the due diligence process is another example that can be frustrating. Circumstances like these can make buying real estate feel like you are on an emotional rollercoaster. During these times, it's important for you to rely on your realtor and his or her objectivity so that you can stay focused on the issues that truly matter most to you.

I've spent quite a bit of time on realtors, but it really is important to have someone on your side of the transaction who is knowledgeable and experienced in real estate and has your best interests in mind. Having someone to guide you through this windy, rocky process will prove to be invaluable.

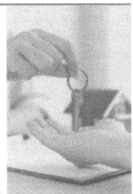

REALTORS

WITH ADDITIONAL NICHE EXPERTISE

1. KNOW ADDITIONAL QUESTIONS TO ASK AND DUE DILIGENCE AREAS
2. CAN BRING ATTENTION TO PROPERTY CHARACTERISTICS THAT MAY NOT FIT YOUR PROPERTY OBJECTIVES
3. WILL SUGGEST OTHER SPECIALIZED RESOURCES TO ASSIST WHEN NEEDED

In addition to those general points, it may also be important for you to seek a realtor who has niche expertise in the area that best aligns with your goals. For example, if you want to purchase a property for the purpose of renting the property on Airbnb as a short-term rental, you may want to find a realtor who specializes in short-term rentals. Why would you need to do that? For starters, that Realtor will know what additional questions to ask to make sure that the properties you're interested in can be used for that specific purpose. They may ask questions like, is the property zoned to use as a short-term rental? Are there changes in the guidelines for short-term rentals that may impact you? Those are just two quick examples of why working with a realtor who has extensive expertise in a specific area of real estate is extremely beneficial.

Number two, Realtors with specialized expertise may also bring attention to property characteristics that do not fit your property objectives. Keeping with the short-term rental example, let's say you want to rent your property out to large groups like bachelorette parties, but the properties you are considering purchasing have only one bathroom or they are away from the city. In a rural setting, your realtor with his or her specialized knowledge would likely guide you to some alternative options that would be a better fit for your goals. Lastly, your realtor can't know everything, but when he or she comes across something that he or she doesn't know, the next best thing is to know who to contact for the information. Realtors who specialize in a particular area network with other key experts in that area, so they know who to turn to when they need additional information.

LENDERS

WHY YOU NEED ONE ON THE DREAM TEAM

1. PROVIDE LENDING EXPERTISE
2. EDUCATE BUYERS
3. PROVIDE LOAN GUIDANCE AND ADVICE
4. OFFER LOAN OPTIONS TO GIVE YOU FINANCIAL LEVERAGE
5. PROVIDE GUIDANCE DURING THE LOAN APPLICATION AND CLOSING PROCESS

Next, let's talk about lenders. I reviewed the awesome benefits of financial leverage in chapter 3. Lenders are awesome resources to have on your real estate dream team because they can guide you through the financial waters and ultimately help you find financing options that fit your needs. Number one, lenders provide lending expertise. Lenders bring tremendous value to the table. Lenders with a high degree of expertise can evaluate your current financial situation and recommend many possible options to address your financing needs. Lending can be a complex process requiring many documents and specific rules of engagement, so you want to work with a lender who is knowledgeable, experienced, caring, and diligent.

Number two, lenders educate buyers. This point resonates deeply with me. I believe the more you know and the better educated you are about lending, the less intimidated you become. Over the years, I have worked with lenders who are willing to answer questions and provide explanations that I can understand. Since you are reading this book and are interested in making money with real estate, whatever investment you make in real estate likely will not be your last. With this in mind, working with a lender who educates you in a way that you can understand is key. Building a basic understanding of financing options and the terminology used will help you become a savvier investor as you mature on your real estate investing journey.

Number three, in addition to the education that lenders provide, they also provide loan guidance and advice. When signing up for a new loan, you'll want to ask lots of questions to understand your options and financial responsibilities. When you're working with a lender to obtain a loan, you may qualify for several options each with their own pros and cons. Because of their expert knowledge and familiarity with the options, lenders can provide guidance and advice so that you can objectively consider all of your options and make the best decision for your unique situation, goals and needs. Number four, as mentioned a few moments ago, lenders offer loan options, and these loan options give you financial leverage. Different lending institutions offer different financing products. It's important to build relationships with lenders at these institutions so you can take advantage of a variety of options to leverage somebody else's money.

Finally, lenders are there to help you navigate the loan application and closing process. I mentioned earlier that purchasing a property can be a very emotional process. There are so many moving parts, and obtaining financing is one of those key components. Lenders provide guidance in the beginning to walk you through the loan application process all the way to closing. There are so many steps, checks, and rechecks as you go through the process of obtaining a loan, and the smoothest way to get through the process is to follow the expert guidance and instructions of a lender. For some people, obtaining the needed financing to purchase a property is something that keeps them from home ownership and investing. With that in mind, I wanted to share some of the key benefits of working with a lender and having one on your dream team. Connect with lenders as a resource to obtain financing when you need money for a real estate transaction. Taking this step can help to ensure lending is not a barrier that keeps you from your real estate ownership goals.

Chapter 5 Activities

Review the chapter questions and enter the answers in the lesson's worksheet in the Ready! Set! Invest! In Real Estate Blueprint

- Reflect on the information provided in this lesson. Based on your specific needs, why do you think you need a Realtor on your real estate dream team?

- Are you currently working with a Realtor? If no, find one this week, add the Realtor's name and contact information to your Blueprint, and contact him or her to make an introduction.

- Based on your specific needs, why do you think you need a lender on your real estate dream team?

- Are you currently working with a lender? If not, find one this week, add the lender's name and contact information to your Blueprint, and contact him or her to make an introduction.

Chapter 6 Property Management: Benefits of having property management companies on your real estate Dream Team

TODAY'S DISCUSSION

OUTLINE OF TOPICS

Property Management

Benefits of having property management companies on your real estate Dream Team

Ready! Set! Invest! in Real Estate | ValeryParham.com

In this chapter, I am going to continue outlining who you should have on your real estate Dream team. The focus of this chapter is property management and the benefits of having a property management company help you with your real estate investment.

PROPERTY MANAGEMENT

WHAT IS PROPERTY MANAGEMENT?

Property management is the daily oversight of residential, commercial, or industrial real estate by a third-party contractor. Generally, property managers take responsibility for day-to-day repairs and ongoing maintenance, security, and upkeep of properties. They usually work for the owners of investment properties.

Their main roles are to manage routine tasks delegated to them by the owners and to preserve the value of the properties they manage while generating income.

- Investopedia

Before I go deeper, I'll review what property management is. Property management is the daily oversight of residential, commercial, or industrial real estate by a third-party contractor. Generally, property managers take responsibility for day-to-day repairs and ongoing maintenance, security, and upkeep of properties. They usually work for the owners of investment properties. Their main roles are to manage routine tasks delegated to them by the owners and to preserve the value of the properties they manage while generating income.

That last sentence should sound like music to your ears. Property managers do all the heavy lifting for you. They handle all of the routine activities required for your rental property to function so that you can make money. Now that you know the basics of what property management is, let's go into more specifics about how property managers can help you from a day-to-day perspective and why you need one on your real estate dream team.

PROPERTY MANAGER

WHY YOU NEED ONE ON THE DREAM TEAM

TENANT MANAGEMENT
- Screen Tenants to acquire and retain higher quality tenants
- Avoid Legal Problems
- Handle Evictions
- Provide 24/7 Guest Support

1

ESTABLISHED SYSTEMS
- Rent Collection Efficiency
- Marketing
- Service Provider relationships

2

PROPERTY BENEFITS
- Fewer Vacancy Periods
- Lower Maintenance and Repair Costs
- Adding Value to Your Rental Properties

3

OWNER ADVANTAGES
- Tax Savings through efficient record-keeping of tax-deductible expenses
- Reduce stress; peace of mind
- Ability to scale to other geographic locations
- More free time & more freedom!

4

I've put the ways property managers can help you into four different categories.

Tenant Management

One of the best things about property managers is they handle all things pertaining to your tenants and your guests. Property managers screen tenants to acquire and retain higher quality tenants. Tenant screening is critical. If you can get the best tenants in the door, make sure that they're paying on time, and make sure that they're taking care of your property, half the battle of rental property ownership is done! As you can see, the screening process is key. Property managers have systems in place to streamline the screening process.

If you have great tenants, you're also probably going to have minimal legal issues or evictions. Good property managers are very well versed in housing laws. They understand the rules of what you can and what you can't do to help you stay within the confines of the law. If there ever does come a time where you need to evict a tenant (hopefully this will never happen to you), property managers know all about the steps, processes and procedures required. Having a property manager in place will help as you navigate these types of situations.

Property managers also handle guest support. When your tenants and guests have an issue, or a general question, they can reach out to your property manager instead of calling and bugging you at all hours of the day and night. Property managers do a great job with tenant management if you have the right property management team in place.

Established Systems

Next, I'll cover systems. Property managers have systems, and they leverage those systems to keep everything associated with your property running smoothly.

Rent collection efficiency is very important for both you and the property manager. Most property management companies operate by collecting a fee for services based on a percentage of the monthly rental rate. This means if you don't make money, they don't make money. This fee structure incentivizes them to make sure that your property is rented, the rent collection process is working seamlessly and that the tenants are paying. Property managers usually have different systems in place so that it's easy for tenants to pay. Tenants get payment reminders with convenient ways to pay.

Property managers are also very skilled at marketing. They can help with tasks like writing descriptions for rental listings, taking high quality photos, and competitively pricing the property. Properties need to be seen to get bookings. Depending on the type of rental, property managers can put your property on multiple websites. These websites could be marketplace websites similar to Airbnb, Apartments.com or Realtor.com. Property managers incorporate high-quality photos in rental listings to appeal to people who are searching for rentals. Many also have tools that suggest pricing based on seasonality, nearby comparable listings, etc. Property managers know how to highlight, market, and price property so it stays booked as much as possible.

Property managers have service provider relationships that really help you in the long run. They usually deal with a large volume of properties. Because property managers give service providers volume, they can get discounts on different types of services. Those discounted fees are passed onto you. Having relationships with service providers who provide services at discounted rates is a phenomenal benefit of having a property manager on your real estate dream team.

Property Benefits

Having property management can directly benefit the property itself. Earlier in the chapter, I mentioned that marketing can drive bookings and reduce vacancy. You want to keep your occupancy rates as high as possible. When you can do that, you stand to make more money. Most costs associated with your rental will be fixed or will only nominally increase with additional bookings. As a result, the revenue you receive from additional bookings will translate into more money in your bank account.

The next in the list is lower maintenance and repair costs. The benefit of lower maintenance and repair costs goes hand in hand with service provider relationships. Obviously, you want to make sure that you keep your property well maintained. Having connections with service providers who are able and available to service your property for any repair or any regular maintenance that's needed is important. Being able to do that at a lower cost is a bonus of using property management.

If you keep your property well maintained over time, you're likely going to be able to benefit from appreciation of your property's value. Property managers can indirectly help add value to your property if they are working with great service providers and keeping your house well maintained.

Owner Advantages

When you work with a property manager, they usually keep very efficient records. Those records usually itemize tax deductible expenses related to keeping your rental property operating. Having itemized expenses will help your tax professional identify applicable tax savings. The more tax savings your tax professional can identify essentially equates to more money that can go back into your pocket around tax time.

Another benefit that may resonate with you is reduced stress and increased peace of mind. I covered tenant management, and the various ways property managers take care of day-to-day activities. If you don't have to worry about calls in the middle of the night, potential legal troubles because you didn't know all of the laws related to fair housing, or vacancy, it can really help reduce your stress. Knowing that you have a property manager who is taking care of these items and more will allow you to focus on other important things like your family or your work.

Having property management in place also gives you the ability to scale. If your goal is to go from your first rental property to your second then your third, having a property management company can help you do this faster and easier. If you want to take advantage of getting some properties in other geographic locations, having property management can help you scale this model too.

Finally, you can have more free time and more freedom if you leverage property managers. If you are not stressed or worried about or actively working on the day-to-day activities related to keeping your property managed, you can use that time to do whatever you want to do with it. The opportunity to make passive income affords you time flexibility and independence, and that is the goal for many of us. Now, let's focus on some additional items that you should consider when you're thinking about selecting a property management company.

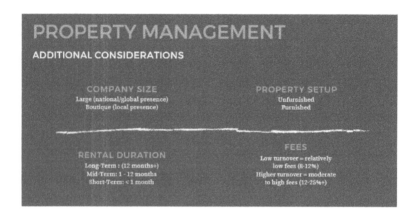

If you need a property management company to manage your property, there are some criteria that you should consider.

Company Size

The first that I have listed is company size. Depending on your goals, you could either have a large company manage your property or a small company handle your property management needs. Large companies can have national or even global presence, and small, boutique companies operate in a local footprint. Given their size differences there are various pros and cons to each. Large companies are going to be able to help you with scale, and they have very streamlined processes. To keep their processes streamlined, they may have a very strict blueprint on how they do things. They may have lots of tools and technology that help them manage property very efficiently, like a well-oiled machine. As you could imaging with larger companies, you sometimes turn into just a number because they have so many other customers. There may also be a need for them to keep things standardized. Because of their large customer base, they can't do one-off services or contract changes to cater to your personal requests or property needs. If they did, they would lose efficiencies in their operating model.

If you need or want more flexibility, you may want to work with a company that has a local presence. There are a lot of benefits that come with working with a smaller company. Local companies may be able to customize services to cater to your specific needs or provide customer service that feels more personal. With local companies, you are more likely to be able to have a main point of contact. You'll be able to call or email this person directly and even meet in person if needed. While working with smaller companies can be great, it can also come with some challenges. For example, smaller companies may not have the same tools or technology as large competitors. Their processes may not be as streamlined as some of the larger companies. These are some example drawbacks of having a boutique or a smaller company from a property management standpoint.

Property Setup

Next, I want to cover the setup of your property. From a high-level, you can setup your property to be an unfurnished or furnished rental. Deciding on an approach will help you identify property management companies that specialize in unfurnished properties or furnished properties. I will go into more details later, but I wanted to introduce the concept as it will play a role when you select a property management company.

Rental duration is another consideration. Do you prefer longer term tenants with leases of 12 months or more? Are you interested in offering a mid-term range lease which could be anything between one and 12 months. Do you want to focus on short-term rentals that could have guest for a few days or a couple weeks? These questions are what you will consider when deciding on the rental duration you want your property to have.

Fees

The last consideration is fee structure. When you have longer leases with lower turnover, it will usually require less work for your property manager. They won't have to service or inspect the property often, so they usually charge lower fees for longer duration bookings. Fees for managing longer durations are relatively low, in the range of about 8% to 12%. Short-term rental on the other hand usually to have high turnover. One group will stay for a couple days. Then another group of people will come for two or three more days. The property management team will have to clean and inspect between bookings. Because of the higher turnover rate, they typically are going to charge you a higher fee. I have seen fees range between 15 to 25%, but the fees could be even more than 25%. It really just depends on the property management company and what they are providing in their services.

Here are two examples of large organizations that provide property management services. Both are in the short-term rental space. The first one is Vacasa. It was established in 2009, and they have a full scope of property management services for vacation type rentals or short-term rentals. They operate in many places including 34 states plus Canada, Mexico, Belize, and Costa Rica. On their website, they tout that they have over 3 million guests per year, 30,000 plus homes, and almost 300,000 5-star reviews on their website.

In comparison, Evolve was conceptualized in 2011. They created a model that enables them to offer a lower fee structure.

Most of Evolve's core services are tied to booking generation. They assist you with marketing the property and acquiring bookings and allow you to select people to clean the property and manage the boots-on-the-ground operations from a local perspective. They tout that they have over 750 destinations, 5 million guests, 15,000 homes, and an average star rating of 4.68.

I hope you have found the information in this chapter helpful as you consider if having a property management company fits within your real estate strategy. Consider the points in this chapter as you continue to build your Blueprint, and make sure to do your own research on property management companies that service your area.

Chapter 6 Activities

Review the chapter questions and enter the answers in the lesson's worksheet in the Ready! Set! Invest! In Real Estate Blueprint located at the end of this book.

- Based on the information provided, what property management benefits are the most important to you?

- Research 3 local property management companies and contact each to learn about their rates and what is included in their rates.

- Review the websites of each of the large property management companies discussed in this chapter then compare the large property management companies with the local property management companies. Which companies appeal to you the most? Why?

Chapter 7 More Dream Team Resources: Additional real estate Dream Team resources to consider adding to your team.

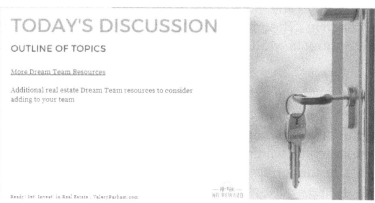

In this chapter, I'll cover a few additional types of resources that you may want to consider adding to your real estate dream team.

Let's first cover resources who you may need during the purchasing process.

Property Inspectors

Property inspectors are extremely important. You should use a property inspector when purchasing a primary residence as well as investment property. A property inspector's job is to inspect a property inside out, from top to bottom. After they inspect a property, they will give you an opinion of the condition of the property based on their findings. They will provide a very detailed, itemized list of all of the issue they found in the property during the inspection process. They'll also give you some indication of the criticality of each item. Armed with this information, you can determine if you want the seller to fix the items in the list or if you want to purchase the property in its as-is state.

Property inspectors also suggest other property concerns that you may want to investigate like wood destroying insects or environmental hazards. In Tennessee, wood destroying insects can cause costly damages to a home. Inspecting for these insects is something you'll want to strongly consider. If you add this service to your overall inspection, the property inspector will advise if he or she sees some indication that the property looks like it has or has had an issue with wood destroying insects. If so, they will also provide guidance on remediation/repair steps.

On the environmental hazard side, inspectors investigate concerns like lead-based paint or asbestos. Depending on the age of your property or other factors, they will recommend additional inspection criteria.

Local Government Contacts

Over the year I have been working on my own properties and rentals, I have really come to appreciate having local government contacts. These contacts include people in your municipality's local building and codes division. They are able to tell you very specific things about what you can or can't do on your property or a property that you're considering purchasing. Local government contacts will give you guidance as to whether or not you are legally permitted to do certain activities at the property's location. Your realtor will likely be able to tell you some of the different rules and regulations from a high level based on zoning, but I also suggest you build your own relationships with these contacts as you acquire more properties and scale. Having someone at the local building department who you can email or call is always very helpful.

For example, if you want to operate a short-term rental in Nashville, TN, you need to confirm that the property's zoning will allow for short-term renting. Depending on the property's zoning, there are certain limitations as to what you can and what you can't do. If you are considering purchasing a property for short-term rentals in Nashville, I highly suggest working with a Realtor who has short-term rental experience. If you also have local government contact who you can ask questions, you can check that the intended rental strategy conforms to the property's zoning regulations.

Insurance Companies (Specialized)

Insurance companies might not be top of mind for everybody in the early stages of acquiring a property. However, if you are thinking about getting into a specialized type of rental like a short-term rental, they should be. Some home insurance companies will not cover that type of intended use. To mitigate risk, research insurance companies during the early stages of your due diligence. Confirm that they will ensure the property given the intended use of the property. For example, your home insurance may cover a fire if the home is owner occupied, but will they cover a fire if it is started by your renters? Confirming that you can get a policy that covers scenarios that could arise given how your property is being used will give you peace of mind.

Business Resources

LAWYERS

- business formation guidance
- long-term business strategy

CERTIFIED PUBLIC ACCOUNT (CPA)

- guidance on business finances
- guidance on applicable tax deductions

BANK

- access to needed funding
- income/expense records separate from your personal finances

72

Now let's go over business resources.

Lawyers

Lawyers can provide guidance on the types of business structure you should consider for your real estate investments. They can also guide you towards other resources you may need for starting a business. They can explain all the details of setting up a business in your state and help you with different types of contracts and legal documents you'll need. Lawyers can also assist with developing a long-term business strategy. Do you plan on adding more properties to your portfolio over time? What about your exit strategy. Develop a relationship with a lawyer and share your overarching real estate plans. You'll want one on your real estate dream team to help you devise a business strategy that supports your end goal.

Certified Public Accountants (CPA)

Just like a lawyer can assist you with certain business aspects like forming a business and planning for the future, a CPA (Certified Public Accountant) is someone who can really help you focus on your finances. You are reading this book because you want to make money from real estate. Making money from real estate is half the battle. The other half is retaining as much of the money you make as possible. That's why having a CPA on your real estate dream team is so important. A CPA can help you manage your finances and find ways to leverage the tax code to your benefit. Finding ways to keep more of your earned dollars in your pockets is a great reason to consider having a CPA on your dream team.

Banking Resources

Earlier, I reviewed mortgage lenders and the importance of having someone on your team who can help you secure financing for buying a property. After obtaining your first property, it's crucial to maintain a relationship with a bank. Having an ongoing relationship with a bank is important because you might need additional funding as part of your overall plan. Banks also offer new products and services all the time. For example, if you want to take out equity from your house or make improvements to your property, a banker can help you find advantageous financing options. Additionally, if you have an investment property and you want to keep your income and expenses separate from your personal finances, having a separate banking institution can be helpful. Keeping your business accounts separate makes managing the financial and accounting aspects of your real estate business easier. Having a solid relationship with banking resources can be clutch for your real estate investing goals.

Property Maintenance Resources

IMPROVEMENTS & MAINTENANCE	CLEANING SERVICES	LAWNCARE SERVICE PROVIDERS
• Ongoing maintenance contractors (handyman) • Building contractors	• Move-in/Move-out/Deep • Laundry Services	• Recurring lawn mowing services • Landscaping

Ready! Set! Invest! in Real Estate | ValeryParham.com

The last group of resources that I'm going review in this chapter are related to ongoing property maintenance.

Improvement/Maintenance Resources

When you have a property, whether it's where you live or an investment property, there will be times when you need maintenance or repairs. To assist with property maintenance and repairs, it's important to find a maintenance person or handyman you trust, who won't charge too much and will do a great job. Of course, you'll have to pay for their services. However, if you don't know much about the work being performed, you might end up paying more than necessary if you are not working with the right person. Finding someone who is skilled, trustworthy, and provides great service without overcharging you is very important.

As your property ventures expand, building contractors become another crucial addition to your team. While the maintenance person may not have the expertise for certain property improvements, building contractors can step in to handle larger building projects. It is essential to have trusted contractors who deliver quality work without overcharging you. This is especially valuable for substantial improvement endeavors like renovations and additions. If these larger-scale projects align with your strategy, it's important to invest time in establishing relationships with reputable contractors.

Cleaning Services

Another critical aspect is cleaning services, which play a significant role in the success of a rental property. Cleaning services can greatly impact the reviews and satisfaction of your guests or tenants when they move in. It is essential to ensure that your properties are always impeccably clean and that the cleaning service pays attention to details. Your reputation is closely tied to the cleanliness of the property when new people move in or out. Therefore, it is vital to have reliable and efficient individuals who can service and clean your property effectively. Another important consideration is the need for additional or specialized services. Depending on the type of rental property strategy you plan to pursue, you may need additional services. For instance, in the case of a furnished, short-term rental, you will need someone to handle laundry tasks before each new guest arrives. This is a quick example of the extra services that may be required based on your rental strategy.

Lawncare Service Providers

Lastly, another aspect that greatly affects the curb appeal of your property is lawn care. Regularly maintaining and caring for your lawn is essential for keeping your property in good condition. It may also entice potential customers to select your property over the competition. Establishing a consistent lawn care routine with a reliable lawncare service provider is vital for overall property maintenance and appeal.

To take your property's curb appeal to the next level, you may also consider including landscaping services. This means that in addition to maintaining the lawn, you could enhance the overall appearance of your property with lush landscaping. It's important to create a positive impression both online and when guests arrive. If you have showcased beautiful landscaping in your property photos, but the actual lawn and shrubbery are neglected when guests arrive, it can harm your reputation. Therefore, it's vital to have landscaping resources on your team to ensure regular upkeep of the property's landscaping in addition to the lawn. These are just a few important considerations to keep in mind.

I hope you found this additional information about essential resources helpful. It's important to note that depending on your strategy, some of these resources may not be necessary. For example, if you have a property manager, you may not need to directly have relationships with some of the resources noted. Property managers often have established relationships with these key resources. However, if you decide not to use a property manager, it is crucial to ensure you have these resources in place. They will assist you in the ongoing care, maintenance, and operations of your rental property investment. Having these resources at a minimum will greatly benefit you.

Chapter 7 Activities

Review the chapter questions and enter the answers in the lesson's worksheet in the Ready! Set! Invest! In Real Estate Blueprint located at the end of this book.

- Based on the information provided, what additional resources do you think you will need on your real estate dream team?

- Research service providers for each of your needs. Remember to check out the resources listed in the Ready! Set! Invest! in Real Estate Resource Guide as well. Which companies/providers are you considering?

- Contact each service provider to learn about their rates and what is included in their rates.

- List the names and contact information of the service providers who you would like to add to your real estate dream team.

SET!

Next, let's get you primed for your next investment by guiding you through additional considerations. This way, when the right investment opportunity presents itself, you can pounce without any hesitation.

Section 3 Make dollars and sense!

Chapter 8 Financial Considerations: Understanding the basic financial considerations & metrics.

If you're like me, you likely want to analyze some numbers before making a large investment in real estate. In this chapter, I will share various financial considerations that you may want to take into account when making real estate investment decisions. How can you determine if an investment opportunity makes sense? Will it be a worthwhile investment? Let's take a look at some key metrics.

SO HOW DO YOU KNOW IF AN INVESTMENT
OPPORTUNITY MAKES SENSE?

LET'S TAKE A LOOK AT
SOME KEY METRICS

When evaluating investment decisions, there are several important metrics to consider. Let's begin by discussing one of them: net operating income.

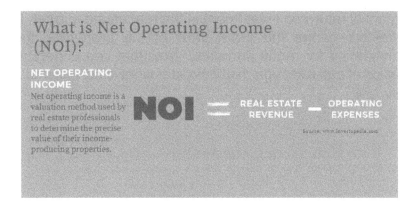

So, what is net operating income (NOI)? Net operating income is a valuation method used by real estate professionals to determine the precise value of income producing properties. To calculate NOI, one must deduct the property's operating expenses from the income it generates.

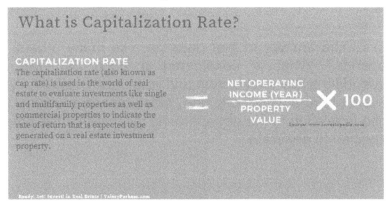

The capitalization rate, commonly referred to as the cap rate, is another metric that investors use when assessing income-producing properties. It is widely utilized in real estate to evaluate various types of investments, such as single-family homes, multi-family properties, and commercial real estate. The cap rate indicates the expected rate of return on an investment property. It is calculated by dividing the net operating income (NOI) - which we discussed earlier - by the property's asset value, and it is expressed as a percentage.

The cap rate is an essential tool for estimating the

potential return on investment in the real estate market. It helps investors gauge the initial yield of the properties they are considering for rental purposes. Now that you understand the basics of cap rate, you might wonder what is considered a good cap rate?

What's a good cap rate?

The answer to that question, like many others, is - "It depends." What is considered a good cap rate varies depending on various factors and your specific goals. Typically, buyers prefer a higher cap rate, which means a lower purchase price in relation to the net operating income that the property is expected to generate.

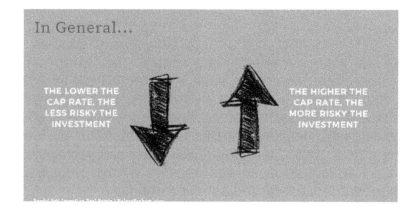

In General...

THE LOWER THE CAP RATE, THE LESS RISKY THE INVESTMENT

THE HIGHER THE CAP RATE, THE MORE RISKY THE INVESTMENT

However, generally speaking, a lower cap rate indicates a less risky investment property, while a higher cap rate suggests a riskier investment. It's important to consider multiple factors when evaluating cap rates. Be sure to discuss this topic with your real estate agent to determine if a property's cap rate is aligned with your goals.

In my personal experience, considering the types of investment opportunities I'm interested in, I typically seek cap rates ranging from 8% to 12%. However, this may not work best for you. It's crucial to analyze each investment opportunity carefully and consider your specific goals, strategy, and risk tolerance. Additionally, it's important to consider factors such as location. Are you purchasing a property in a bustling city like New York or in a rural area of Tennessee? The asset class should also be taken into account. Are you buying a multifamily property or a single-family residence? These types of factors can influence the cap rate.

It's also worth considering the available inventory in the area. If the inventory is limited, it could drive up prices and result in a lower cap rate. Remember, cap rates are relative, so it's advisable to discuss your goals with a Realtor. They can provide insights on cap rates in the areas you're interested in and compare them with the cap rates of properties you're considering. This will give you a better understanding of how your desired properties align with the prevailing cap rates.

An additional metric that you may also evaluate is cash-on-cash return. According to Investopedia, "a cash-on-cash return is a rate of return often used in real estate transactions that calculates the cash income earned on the cash invested in a property." This simply means cash-on-cash return is a measure of the cash flow a property generates relative to the amount of money invested to create that cash flow. To help illustrate cash-on-cash return, consider this example. You purchase a duplex for $500,000. You make a downpayment of $125,000 and get a loan for the remaining $375,000. You decide to charge $1500 in rent per month for both units of the duplex. At the end of your first year of owning the property, you paid $24,000 in mortgage payment and $10,000 in maintenance and miscellaneous expenses. Both units of your property were rented for 10 months so you received $30,000 in rental income. Of those payments, $2500 contributed to reducing your principal on the loan. Let's say you decide to sell the property at the end of one year of ownership, and you are able to sell the property for $525,000. Considering this scenario, your total cash invested would be $159,000. The property generated $30,000 throughout the year and after paying off the remaining loan balance of $372,500, you made $152,500 from the sale of the property. In this simple example, you as the investor would have a cash-on cash return of ($182,500 − $159,000)/$159,000 = 14.8%

Another quick and easy calculation that you may consider is the 1% rule. The 1% rule provides a simple, high-level estimate of the minimum amount of rent that you would want to charge for an investment property. Calculating minimum rents using the 1% rule is easy. Simply multiply the purchase price of the potential investment property by 1% or move the decimal point 2 places to the left. As a quick example, consider you are searching for properties and come across a $525,000 property that you really like. If you applied the 1% rule to estimate the minimum rent you would need to charge, you the result would be $5,250 per month. If your additional research suggests that's a reasonable rent for comparable properties in the area, then the investment could be worth continued evaluation. If not, you may decide to pass on the opportunity and continue searching for others that would be more profitable.

Now that you're familiar with some important metrics, let's review additional factors to consider when thinking creatively about investment opportunities. While it's essential to ensure that any investments you're considering are financially viable, it's equally important to evaluate if these opportunities align with your personal goals, lifestyle, and desired real estate investing strategy.

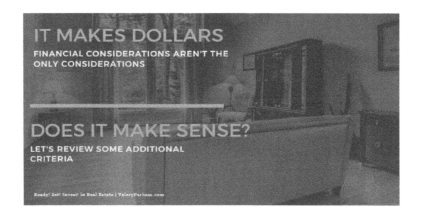

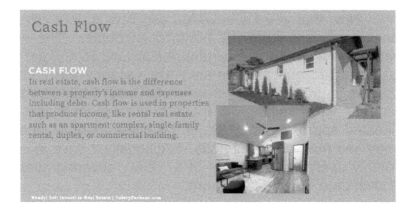

Keeping that in mind, let's dig into the topic of cash flow in real estate. Cash flow is the difference between a property's income and expenses inclusive of debts. Cash flow is used to evaluate properties that produce income such as rental real estate. Examples include apartment complexes, single family rentals, duplexes or commercial buildings. Positive cash flow occurs when the income generated from a property surpasses the expenses and financing costs, while negative cash flow arises when the expenses and financing costs exceed the income.

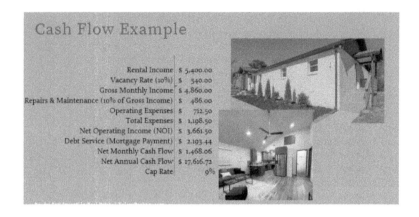

Cash Flow Example

Rental Income	$ 5,400.00
Vacancy Rate (10%)	$ 540.00
Gross Monthly Income	$ 4,860.00
Repairs & Maintenance (10% of Gross Income)	$ 486.00
Operating Expenses	$ 712.50
Total Expenses	$ 1,198.50
Net Operating Income (NOI)	$ 3,661.50
Debt Service (Mortgage Payment)	$ 2,193.44
Net Monthly Cash Flow	$ 1,468.06
Net Annual Cash Flow	$ 17,616.72
Cap Rate	9%

Now that you know what cash flow is, let's consider a specific example from my portfolio—a duplex. The average rental rates for this property generate around $5,400 per month. Taking into account an estimated 10% vacancy rate, I anticipate an average gross monthly income of at least $4,860 throughout this year. Now, shifting our focus to the expense side, I have allocated approximately 10% of the gross monthly income for repair and maintenance needs. Additionally, I have factored in monthly operating expenses of $712.50, covering items such as lawn care, utilities, and more.

The total monthly expense for the expense items noted above is $1,198.50. Subtracting the total monthly expenses of $1,198.50 from the gross monthly income of $4,860 results in net operating income of $3,661.50.

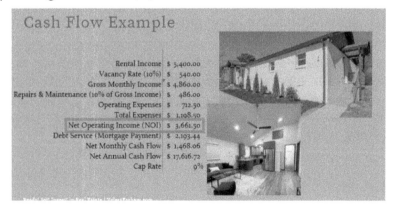

Cash Flow Example

Rental Income	$ 5,400.00
Vacancy Rate (10%)	$ 540.00
Gross Monthly Income	$ 4,860.00
Repairs & Maintenance (10% of Gross Income)	$ 486.00
Operating Expenses	$ 712.50
Total Expenses	$ 1,198.50
Net Operating Income (NOI)	$ 3,661.50
Debt Service (Mortgage Payment)	$ 2,193.44
Net Monthly Cash Flow	$ 1,468.06
Net Annual Cash Flow	$ 17,616.72
Cap Rate	9%

Next to arrive at the net monthly cash flow of $1,468.06, deduct the monthly mortgage payment of $2,193.44 from the net operating income of $3,661.50. To get the net annual cash flow, multiply the net monthly cash flow by 12. In this example, the net annual cash flow is $17,616.72.

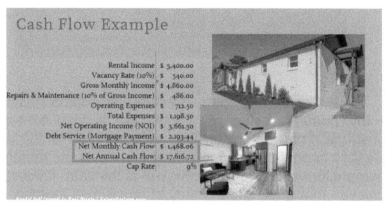

After you obtain the net annual cash flow for the property, you can determine the cap rate. The cap rate estimated for this property's given the assumptions noted is 9%. To calculate the cap rate for this example, simply divide the net annual cash flow of $17,616.72 by the property's value of $475,000 and multiply by 100 to get a percentage. Based on the cap rate range that I target for my investments, this property's cap rate of 9% falls within that desired range. This property works for me, but would this opportunity be attractive to you?

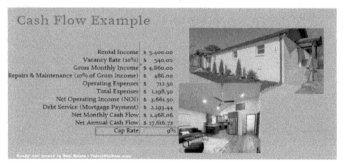

Let's consider another scenario. I introduced you to my first rental property earlier in the program's content.

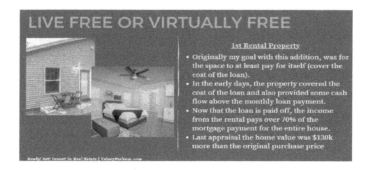

My first rental property is actually an addition that I added to my primary residence. I obtained a loan to fund the construction of this addition. Originally, my goal for this addition was for it to generate enough income to cover the monthly loan payment for at least nine months out of the year. It successfully achieved that goal, and in many of those nine months, it even generated additional cash flow beyond the loan payment. In a few years, I paid off the loan in full. Now that the loan has been paid, income from the addition contributes a significant amount towards my monthly mortgage payment. This excites me! Additionally, since adding the additional square footage to the home, the property's value has increased over a hundred thousand dollars based on the most recent appraisal.

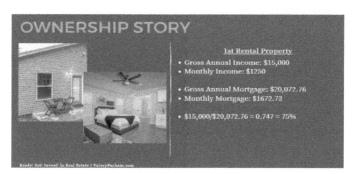

Upon reviewing the annualized figures, the additional 350 square feet of living space that I added to my home generated $15,000 in income. This amount covered nearly 75% of my current monthly mortgage payment. I find this to be incredible because it means I am now only paying approximately $420 each month to live in my house. This is 75% less than what I previously had to spend from my earned income.

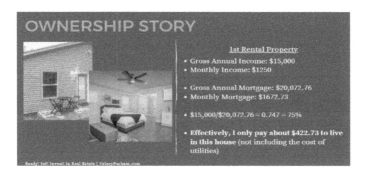

OWNERSHIP STORY

1st Rental Property
- Gross Annual Income: $15,000
- Monthly Income: $1250

- Gross Annual Mortgage: $20,072.76
- Monthly Mortgage: $1672.73

- $15,000/$20,072.76 = 0.747 = 75%

- **Effectively, I only pay about $422.73 to live in this house** (not including the cost of utilities)

At this point, I hope that these examples have sparked your interest in exploring your own goals and the opportunities available to you. However, before you rush into purchasing a property, let's go over some additional factors to consider. For example, what happens if you purchase a property, and you can't find renters for your property? I personally experienced this situation when the Covid 19 pandemic hit the United States and sent shockwaves through the travel industry.

What happens if you can't find renters for your property?

When the Covid-19 pandemic started, I was operating the addition as an Airbnb rental on a short-term basis. Due to strict lockdown measures and travel restrictions, Airbnb implemented a policy that allowed all travelers to cancel their bookings. As a result, property owners like me saw fully booked calendars evaporate in an instant.

How to Handle Vacancy

If you ever find yourself in a situation where you don't have renters for your property, it's essential not to panic. Instead, it's wise to prepare for such scenarios before they strike. How can you handle a vacancy at your property? Here are a few suggestions:

1. **Don't bite off more than you can chew**. Make sure that you are not overextending yourself on any new investment opportunity that you are considering. It is crucial to assess whether you can afford to make payments on your investment for a reasonable period, even if you do not have a renter. This timeframe could range from three to six months or more. It is important to be confident that you can cover the payments after acquiring a property.

2. **Build a solid reserve.** It is important to build a strong reserve fund in case of emergencies, such as extended vacancies. Instead of immediately paying yourself profits from the property, consider allowing the profits to accumulate in a separate account designated for unforeseen challenges and difficult times. By doing so, you will have a financial cushion to cover monthly

property expenses during unexpected circumstances and proverbial rainy days. This reserve account will serve as a safeguard and provide peace of mind during challenging periods.

3. **Know when to pivot.** I previously shared how the pandemic affected my rental. In 2020 after the Corona virus spread to the United States, I experienced a complete loss of all bookings, which resulted in no rental income during the second quarter of the year. However, I still had to make the loan payment each month. During that time, I had to cover both the mortgage payment and the improvement loan payment from my personal funds. Given the uncertainty of the situation, no one knew when travel would resume. Faced with so much uncertainty, I needed to explore alternative opportunities to make money from the rental aside from my Airbnb strategy. After enduring several months without rental income, I decided to shift to a month-to-month rental agreement. The pivot in strategy thankfully provided a consistent source of income until travel restrictions were lifted for vacationers.

This example from my personal experience serves to highlight the importance of being adaptable and switching strategies when necessary. When challenging situations arise, the goal is to do whatever is necessary to cover your property's expenses until you are able to resume generating income. However, it is crucial to remember that you can also make a pivot and sell the property if absolutely necessary. Evaluate your options carefully and make the decision that is best for you.

There are numerous ways to approach and assess your options if you experience extended periods of unexpected vacancies. It's essential to consider the specifics of your situation to find the options that best suit your needs.

Chapter 8 Activities

Review the chapter questions and enter the answers in the lesson's worksheet in the Ready! Set! Invest! In Real Estate Blueprint located at the end of this book.

- Review NOI and capitalization rate. Did you know about these financial metrics? Did you know how to calculate them? Do you still have questions? If so, what questions do you have?

- Prior to this lesson, had you considered being able to live for free or virtually free or generating a positive cash flow from your real estate investments? How would living free or virtually free change your life? How would generating a positive cash flow change your life?

- Had you previously considered what to do if you have a vacancy for an extended period of time? Which option(s) presented resonated with you most? What other options can you think of?

Chapter 9 Creative Options: Creative Options to Help You Get Started with Making Money with Real Estate

In everyday conversations about investing in real estate, you've probably heard people say things like you should have at least 20% down on a home. While having a sizeable downpayment for a property comes with benefits, it is daunting for many people to save such a large percentage of a property's sales price.

With this in mind, I will cover some creative options for getting started in real estate in this chapter.

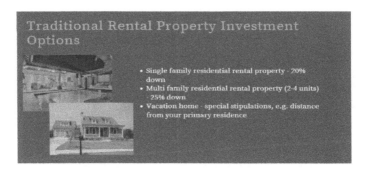

Before exploring alternative options, let's briefly review some traditional paths to real estate investing. It's important to note that there is absolutely nothing wrong with any of these options. They are simply more conventional routes to acquiring investment property and are often what people think of when it comes to real estate investment requirements. I mention these options strictly to establish a baseline for comparison with the creative options I will present in this chapter. When contemplating the purchase of investment properties, you might consider the following traditional options:

Purchasing a single-family investment property. If you intend to buy a single-family residence as an investment property, it is typically expected that you provide a down payment of at least 20% of the property's purchase price.

Purchasing a multi-family investment property. If you are considering a multi-unit property for investment purposes, you will generally need to provide a down payment of around 25% or more.

Purchasing a vacation home. If you are interested in buying a vacation home, it is typically required to have a down payment of at least 10% to 15% of the property's purchase price.

Remember, these traditional options serve as a foundation for comparison as we explore more creative approaches to real estate investment in the remainder of this chapter.

NOW, LET'S REVIEW

SOME MORE
CREATIVE OPTIONS

With a high-level understanding of the traditional options established, let's review some more creative alternatives. It's time to start thinking outside the box. To kick off the list of non-traditional options, let's start with "house hacking." House hacking involves purchasing a multi-unit property and living in one of the units while renting the remaining units. The concept of house hacking first crossed my mind when I was living in my first house. Even before I knew there was a term for it, I had considered house hacking but never to action. Then in 2017, while returning from a trip to Greece, I chatted with a gentleman who sat next to me on the plane. After some initial small talk, he shared his personal journey of how he started from very humble beginnings and eventually became a millionaire.

He shared that what truly set him on the path to success was house hacking. He started by purchasing a quadplex, a property with four units, and living in one unit while renting out the others. He used the rental income to expedite the mortgage paydown. Once he paid off the property completely, he repeated the process by purchasing another quadplex. He continued this cycle, building a portfolio and business worth over $10,000,000. Yes, read the number correctly. The number 10 followed by 6 zeros - $10 million dollars. After hearing his inspiring story, I knew I wanted to start house hacking in some capacity.

Now, let's move on to the next creative option, the "house hop hack." Try to say that three times fast. While it may be a slight tongue twister, bear with me as I review the strategy. With this strategy, you purchase a house as your primary residence. When you are ready to move out and purchase another property to live in, instead of selling your original house, you keep it and rent it out. By doing so, you are able to move to your next house without the need to invest a sizable down payment. The key to successful house hopping is to continue living within your means when purchasing the subsequent house.

Lastly, another strategy worth mentioning is adding additional space to your primary residence and using the added square footage as a rental. This option is nice for those who prefer to start small and reasonably estimate that adding extra space will increase the value of their home. If your home already has some equity, you could consider using that equity to fund the construction of the addition.

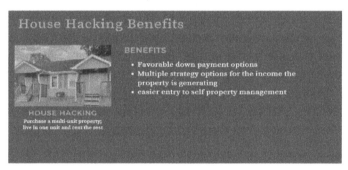

Now you understand the concept of house hacking, but what are some benefits of house hacking? First, you are likely to have favorable down payment options since you are purchasing the property for the purpose of living in it. This can dramatically reduce the initial financial investment required to obtain the property. Next, you will have several options regarding the use of the rental income the property is generating. You can choose to use the income to make additional payments on the property to accelerate paying off the mortgage. Alternatively, you can save the rental income for unexpected expenses or future investments. Another option is to use the rental income to cover the mortgage payments, effectively allowing you to live in the property for free or at a significantly reduced cost. Lastly, since the rental unit is physically connected to the unit you are living in, it provides a more convenient, straightforward entry into self-property management. This means you can try your hand at being a landlord and managing the property yourself, gaining valuable experience and potentially saving on property management costs.

Next, let's explore the benefits of leveraging the house hop hack strategy. If you already own a primary residence, you are in a potentially perfect position to try the house hop hack. With this strategy, you can even leave your existing furniture in the house you're going to rent to quickly convert it to a furnished rental. Additionally, as mentioned before, you will have access to more favorable down payment options since you are moving into the new home for the purpose of living in it. If you have built equity in your primary residence, any available equity can be used to help finance or make improvements to the home you are moving to, thus potentially enhancing its value. Furthermore, as discussed earlier, you have several options for using the rental income generated by the property you converted into a rental.

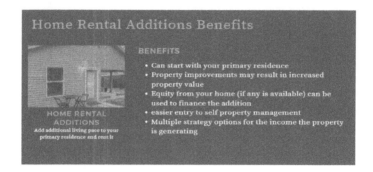

Home Rental Additions Benefits

BENEFITS
• Can start with your primary residence
• Property improvements may result in increased property value
• Equity from your home (if any is available) can be used to finance the addition
• easier entry to self property management
• Multiple strategy options for the income the property is generating

HOME RENTAL ADDITIONS
Add additional living pace to your primary residence and rent it

What about the benefits of a home additional used as a rental? With a home addition, you can start with your primary residence if you are already a homeowner. One significant advantage is that property improvements may result in an increase in your property's value. Similar to the house hop hack scenario, if you have built equity in your home, you may be able to use that equity to finance the construction of the addition. Since a home addition is another way to get into a position to house hack, building an addition to rent provides an easy entry to self-property management since the rental space is attached to your home. Just like the other two options we discussed; you also have several options for using the income generated by the addition. For instance, you can choose to make additional payments on the mortgage. Alternatively, you can use the rental income to cover a portion or all of your housing expenses. If the rental income is enough to completely cover your housing expenses, you will effectively live in the house for free.

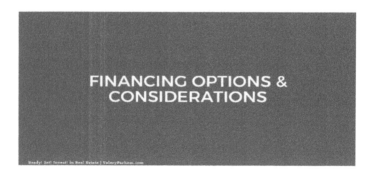

FINANCING OPTIONS & CONSIDERATIONS

Ready! Set! Invest! in Real Estate | ValeryParhm.com

Financing options

We've reviewed some creative property investment options. Let's now shift to financing those options. There are many potential financing options so for simplicity I will introduce four for you to consider.

Mortgage

First, there's the mortgage option. There are several types of mortgages including conventional, FHA, and VA. Each of the types has different requirements and stipulations of the loan. For instance, some mortgages must be used for purchasing a primary residence while others can be used for investment purposes. Depending on the intended use of the loan, down payment terms could be as low as 0% to 20% or more.

The next option is a home equity loan. This type of loan is backed by the equity in your home. It is distributed for use as a lump sum, which you repay in regular installments over a specified period of time.

HELOCs, or home equity lines of credit, are also secured by the equity in your home. However, they differ from home equity loans in that they function more like a credit card. With a HELOC, you have access to a maximum limit of funds that you can use as needed in any amount up to your maximum available amount. This option offers lots of flexibility in borrowing funds for your investment endeavors.

Finally, let's discuss home improvement loans. Unlike home equity loans or HELOCs, home improvement loans can be unsecured, which means they are not backed by your home's equity. These loans provide you with a lump sum of money that you repay through regular installment payments. Over time, a home improvement loan can be used to implement the home addition strategy we discussed in this lesson. It offers a way to finance the costs associated with making improvements to your property without using the equity in your home as collateral.

Each of these financing options has its own considerations and requirements. It's important to thoroughly evaluate and compare them to determine which option aligns best with your investment goals and financial situation.

Chapter 9 Activities

Review the chapter questions and enter the answers in the lesson's worksheet in the Ready! Set! Invest! In Real Estate Blueprint located at the end of this book.

- Of the rental property investment options (traditional and creative) presented in this lesson, which seems like the route you would most likely take? If you have another route, you have been considering, please list that option in your answer.

- Of the financing options discussed, which seem like options you would like to consider for your entry into your investment property? What questions do you have about these options?

Section 4 Niche Rental Income Options

Chapter 10 Know Your Niche: Time to explore some niche property rental options

For those ready to explore purchasing their first or next rental opportunity, let's review some different niche options to consider.

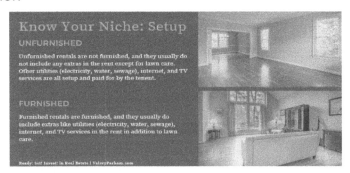

The first thing to consider is the setup of your property. When thinking about rental properties, two basic types of setups come to mind: unfurnished and furnished. Unfurnished properties do not come with furnishings, and they usually do not include utilities, TV services, or internet. Typically, renters will need to furnish the rental and set up their own electricity, water, internet, and any additional monthly services. In contrast, furnished properties come with furnishings such as couches, televisions, and beds. They also usually include extras like utilities, electricity, water, and internet services. Furnished rentals appeal to vacationers and renters who are looking for extra convenience.

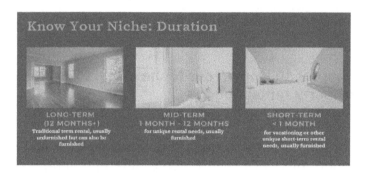

After considering the setup of your property, you also want to think about the duration of the tenant's stay. When thinking about traditional rental properties, tenants typically stay for at least several months. For long-term rentals, you would provide a lease with a duration of 12 months or more. Long-term rentals are convenient because you don't have to deal with frequent turnover if your tenant is content. Properties set up for longer-term use are usually unfurnished and do not include any extras. Tenants bring their own furnishings and establish their own accounts for utilities, electricity, internet services, etc.

Some tenants need space for a period that is less than 12 months but longer than a few days. These renters require a mid-term duration stay, usually somewhere between 1 month and 12 months. Because renters with mid-term needs are staying for a relatively short time, they prioritize convenience. If they're only staying for a month, three months, or six months, they don't want to bring in their own furniture or deal with setting up utilities. Therefore, you will need to provide a furnished, turnkey rental for renters seeking a mid-term stay.

There's one final duration to cover: short-term. There are some people who only need to use your space for a few days or weeks. Any stay duration of less than 1 month is considered a short-term rental. Many people associate short-term rentals with Airbnb. With short-term rentals, guests are likely visiting an area for vacation or a specific event like a concert or work. These renters also need the convenience of a fully furnished, turnkey property, and they are looking for an alternative to a hotel. Guests may want a unique ambiance to complement their occasion. A person traveling for work during the week has different needs from a group traveling for a bachelorette party weekend. For these reasons, it's important to have an idea of what type of atmosphere you want to provide to attract your ideal renters.

Let's compare the various duration options so you can better understand each and why you may choose one over another. Of the three options, setting up a long-term rental requires the lowest cost of entry because you don't have to furnish the property. As mentioned earlier, the tenant is responsible for furnishing the property. The tenant is usually also responsible for setting up and paying the utilities and other month-to-month expenses associated with living there. One minor challenge with long-term rentals is you will have less frequent visibility to damage or issues caused by the tenant. This challenge is a result of long-term rentals having low or infrequent turnover. Some rental property owners are willing to accept this risk because they prefer the more passive nature of longer-term leases. Infrequent turnover can be seen as both a positive and a negative depending on your goals as a rental property owner. Lastly, relative to the other options, your gross income will typically be on the lower end of that spectrum. This is because your property is not set up to offer extra amenities and convenience like furnished rentals. Without extras and added convenience, you will not be able to charge higher rents for the space.

When considering a mid-term property rental strategy, the upfront costs are higher because you usually need to furnish the property. As the owner, you will be responsible for utilities and other expenses associated with the operation of the property. You will have a bit more visibility to any damage because tenant leases are turning over every few months. You will have more visibility than you would have with a long-term rental but less visibility than you would have with a short-term rental. The turnover frequency for mid-term rentals is in the middle of the spectrum. Mid-term rentals have more turnover than rentals with a long-term setup. However, they have less turnover than a property with a short-term setup. The relative gross income opportunity for mid-term rentals typically falls somewhere between long-term and short-term rentals.

For short-term rentals, you will have upfront furnishing costs. You'll be responsible for covering the cost of the utilities and the other property expenses. There will be a lot of opportunities to check in and look at your property. Every time a tenant enters or exits the property, you or your property manager will have a chance to inspect the property. Therefore, if there are any issues, you're able to address them quickly to keep the property well maintained. Turnover for short-term rentals tends to be on the higher side. If your short-term rental property is generating a lot of activity, you will have higher turnover rates. High turnover is to be expected because people are coming in for a few days and leaving. Short-term rentals that are in prime locations, provide a unique experience, being in a prime location, and offer great amenities and convenience have a greater opportunity to generate higher gross income relative to the other options.

After you decide on a setup and duration, you will need to determine how to market your property so you can get renters. For traditional, unfurnished, long-term rentals, you may opt to use a site like Realtor.com or hire a property manager to list and market your property. For mid-term and short-term rentals, you may decide to use marketplace to list your property. What are these niche marketplaces where you can list your short- and mid-term properties and gain visibility? One of the first ones that usually comes to everybody's mind is Airbnb. Airbnb's been around since 2007. It's primarily a short-term rental marketplace that focuses on unique stays and one-of-a-kind activities and experiences. It's grown to over 4 million hosts who have welcomed more than 1 billion guests from every country across the globe. Its global reach is truly remarkable. If you are considering getting into that short-term rental space, Airbnb is definitely a platform to consider for marketing to its vast userbase.

The next platform I'd like to highlight is Furnished Finder. I have personally used it for mid-term rentals, and it has been a valuable tool to market to and find tenants. Furnished Finder was started in 2014. It's a short-term and mid-term housing marketplace that specifically targets travel nurses and other business travelers who need furnished housing. Furnished Finder boasts that they have this 92-day average stay, making it an attractive option for those seeking accommodations for around 3 months. Furnish Finders also provides data and resources for corporate housing coordinators and medical staffing companies across the United States. If you are looking to attract nurses and other business travelers, Furnished Finder may be a great place to list your property.

Now that you have an overview of these two marketplaces, let's review some pros and cons of each.

When considering Airbnb, it's important to note that visitors to the platform are primarily searching for short-term rentals. This presents a great opportunity for your property to gain visibility among visitors who are looking for space in your area. Airbnb offers lots of tools designed to help you maximize your profits. Their price adjustment feature is an example of one notable tool. This feature works by automatically adjusting your listing's daily rate depending on demand in your area. Variables that impact demand include seasons or special events in your area. For example, if a highly anticipated concert comes to your area during the summer months, Airbnb can increase your daily rental rate without your manual intervention. This automated pricing system can significantly enhance your ability to maximize the profits you can generate.

Airbnb also has seamless systems. One key example payment collection via Airbnb. Airbnb's systems make it easy to create a listing and include instructions for guests to access and use the property. You can create and provide information for guests like guidebooks highlighting local restaurants or things to do in the area. Once you have completely set up your Airbnb listing, the rental process for you and your guests is very intuitive and smooth.

While Airbnb has many benefits, there are some drawbacks to the platform. One notable restriction is you are not able to have a conversation with your guests prior to making the commitment to allow them to stay in the property. Airbnb has tools that allow you to message potential guests within the Airbnb platform. However, if you want to have a phone conversation with somebody, Airbnb does not allow that type of interaction prior to both parties committing to the booking. This can be limiting when you want to make sure your property meets the needs of potential guests before confirming their stay. Additionally, Airbnb generates additional revenue by adding fees to the rental rates you set for your listing. These fees stacked onto your rental rates and applicable taxes can make your listing appear to be more expensive than other listings. Finally, Airbnb commands lots of visitor traffic, but there's also significant competition. Due to the high number of properties listed, Airbnb can be a crowded marketplace for property owners. This high level of competition is worth considering when deciding to use Airbnb.

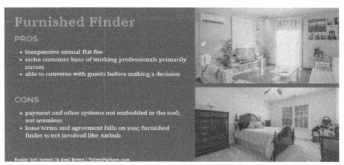

There are several aspects of Furnished Finder that make it a great option to consider for furnished rentals. One standout feature of Furnish Finder is its annual flat fee that is extremely affordable. When I initially subscribed to list on Furnish Finder, the fee was only $99 per year per property listed. Whether you generate $30,000 a year or $50,000 a year, the only fee you pay Furnished Finder is the annual $99 flat fee. Furnished Finder does not have as many bells and whistles as Airbnb, but its simple, low fee structure is unbeatable.

As mentioned earlier, Furnish Finder's customer base mainly consists of working professionals, primarily nurses. Being directly connected to this customer base was particularly beneficial during the challenges brought on by the Covid-19 pandemic. During the pandemic, nurses and other medical professionals were allowed to travel for work, and they needed turnkey accommodations for their visits. Having property listed on Furnished Finder ensures that you have access to renters in high demand, critical professions who require temporary housing arrangements for work. This niche of potential renters can provide a stable stream of income. For this reason, Furnish Finder is a strong rental marketplace option to consider.

Lastly, in contrast to Airbnb, you can talk with your guests before either of you make a final decision on the booking. Furnished Finder allows the guests to provide their phone number. You can text or call potential guests, and vice versa. This direct communication facilitates a better understanding of their preferences and needs. It also helps both parties gain a level of comfort with each other before confirming a booking.

Using Furnished Finders does have a couple of drawbacks to consider. First, Furnished Finder does not have robust, integrated systems. For example, you will need to use another program to collect payments from your tenants.

Also, unlike Airbnb, Furnished Finder does not act as an intermediary between you and tenants. With Furnished Finder, you must set up lease agreements with your tenants. Disagreements and disputes with tenants must be handled directly because each party has a direct contractual relationship with the other, not the marketplace. Make sure you take this into consideration when using Furnished Finder.

Other Websites & Marketplaces

Before concluding this chapter, I'd like to share a few other places where you can list your property. The first one is Avail.co. Avail.co is a website that is affiliated with Realtor.com. One great benefit of using Avail.co to list your property is Avail.co will automatically push your listing to Realtor.com and other top rental listing websites. Realtor.com is a popular online resource where people go to look for properties to rent or buy. By listing your property on Avail.co, your property becomes accessible to potential renters browsing Realtor.com and other sites. The added exposure increases the potential for your property to be seen and rented.

Another marketplace worth considering is Facebook Marketplace. Almost everyone has a Facebook account, so Facebook Marketplace is another online resource that has a large user base. Facebook Marketplace has a category that allows users to search for rentals in their area. This makes Facebook Marketplace a viable option for listing your rental property.

In addition to Facebook Marketplace, I want to mention Facebook Groups. You can search Facebook groups created for people who are looking for places to stay in your area. It's straightforward and simple to find these groups by searching for keywords like "rental properties" or "rental properties in [your city]." After you find a group, request to join the group. Once you've been accepted, you can participate in conversations, see who's looking for property, and potentially share your listing with that group members for their consideration.

Chapter 10 Activities

Review the chapter questions and enter the answers in the lesson's worksheet in the Ready! Set! Invest! In Real Estate Blueprint located at the end of this book.

- Based on the information presented in this lesson, which rental setup and duration appeal to you most as starting points for your property rental?

- Are you considering using marketplace sites like Airbnb or Furnished Finder? If so, which marketplaces appeal to you most? Which are you least interested in?

- Are you interested in other property rental websites that were not covered in this lesson? If so, please list those websites, and describe why you are interested in them.

Chapter 11 Additional Niche Options: Non-residential use location rentals

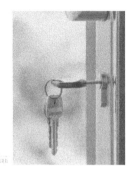

In the last chapter, we covered residential use property rentals. Now we will explore niche options for non-residential use property rentals.

You might be wondering, "What exactly are non-residential use rentals?" To clarify, I will start by explaining what residential use rentals are. Residential rentals are for individuals seeking a place to live. These rental spaces are used to carry out their daily activities like rest, relaxation, and so on.

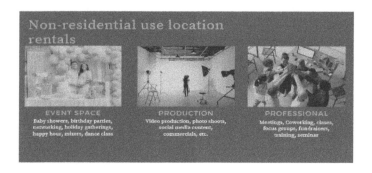

Non-residential use location rentals, on the other hand, encompass a full spectrum of possibilities. I'll focus on three key non-residential use property rental categories to consider: event space, production activities, and professional settings and meetings.

Let's start with event space. Using your property as event space could entail hosting various events like baby showers, birthday parties, holiday gatherings, or mixers. If you can create a versatile space that caters to various renter themes and color preferences, your property could be used for hosting events. Hosting events and gatherings might be another way for you to leverage your property beyond traditional residential uses to generate income.

Another option is using your rental for production activities. Production activities encompass individuals or companies using your space to film movies and commercials, conduct photo shoots, create social media content, or film YouTube videos. If you have adequate space and you include the necessary equipment and features conducive for production activities, this non-residential use option can be a profitable use for your rental property.

Finally, your property could be used as a location for professional activities. Individuals and business owners often need space to conduct business related activities. These individuals may need meeting space, co-working areas, or locations to host training meetings, workshops, or seminars. Your rental property could be the perfect space to facilitate these activities. If your property includes open areas conducive to gatherings and collaboration, offering it as a space for professional activities and meetings could be another excellent way to generate income.

Now, let's explore some of the benefits and considerations of using your property for non-residential rental purposes. From a benefits perspective, you might have the opportunity to charge higher rates for your property. One way you can achieve this is by breaking up the day into hour blocks. Doing so will allow you to accommodate more clients per day so you can boost daily revenues. Your pricing structure could also be based on daily rates, event-specific pricing or by contract. With these various structures, you may be able to host special events or retreats for larger groups and command higher prices for your space.

Multiple factors should be considered when determining the pricing of your property. Use type and duration of use are two major factors. Durations could range from a few days to weeks or even months. For instance, in the case of a movie production with large crews and the need for a significant amount of space, you may have the opportunity to charge thousands or even tens of thousands of dollars for the use of your property.

Now that you understand some of the benefits of non-residential use location rentals, let's review some key considerations. The first one is the size of your space. If you plan to host large groups, you'll need to make sure that your property can accommodate them. Additionally, determine if there are special furnishings or features are required like lighting for photo shoots, high-speed Wi-Fi for meetings, or other specialized amenities. These types of considerations become crucial when your plan for your property goes beyond the typical residential use.

Additionally, you need to make sure that there aren't any rules or regulations that permit you from renting the property using these alternative options. Check your local municipality rules to ensure there aren't property zoning limitations permitting these or other uses that you are considering. Also check your homeowner's association (HOA) rules if you have one to confirm your HOA permits the identified property rental use. It's imperative to verify your property's governing entities allow the intended use if you plan on implementing some of these creative ways to use your property.

Example non-residential use location rental marketplaces

You're now acquainted with the concept of non-residential use rentals. Now, I would like to share some examples of marketplaces that cater to non-residential uses. This list is not exhaustive but is intended to provide a few starting places for you to explore.

The first example is really going to resonate with those who enjoy making music and are in the Music City or one similar to Nashville. It's called Studio Time. Studio Time is an online marketplace created for people who have equipped their properties with recording studio equipment for recording music songs, and related activities. People in search of a recording studio can visit Studio Time to find and book studios that are available in their area.

Next on the list is Peer Space. Peer Space is a marketplace that primarily concentrates on meeting spaces suitable for content creation and celebrations. I reviewed the option to use your rental space for meetings, professional purposes, and events earlier. If using your space for these activities is of interest to you, Peer Space might be a platform worth exploring.

Spacey is another platform to consider. Spacey's marketplace specializes in events, filming, and photo shoots. If you have a creative eye or knack for design and believe your space would accommodate these purposes, Spacey could be a great resource for you to list your property.

Rounding out the list is Giggster. This marketplace is dedicated to spaces suitable for filming and events. If your space is unique and has a cinematic appeal perfect for movies, commercials, and similar projects, visit Giggster to learn more.

These are just a few quick examples of marketplaces for you to review. There are numerous marketplaces available so do your research to discover other creative, non-residential use rental marketplaces. Depending on the rental use you want to pursue, you can likely find a rental marketplace that caters to your desired clientele.

Armed with these creative examples for alternate uses of your rental property and marketplaces to investigate, I hope you are encouraged by the many possibilities of your space. Stay curious and research additional ways your property can generate income. You may be surprised by the multitude of options.

Chapter 11 Activities

Review the chapter questions and enter the answers in the lesson's worksheet in the Ready! Set! Invest! In Real Estate Blueprint located at the end of this book.

- Prior to listening to this lesson, were you familiar with non-residential use location rentals?

- After listening to this lesson, would you consider this use for your rental property or are you more interested in traditional residential rental property uses?

- If you are interested in non-residential use location rentals, what type interests you most? e.g. meetings, events, production?

Section 5 Building Systems

Chapter 12 Property Management vs Self-Management: Consider using property management companies or self-managing

After you select the rental use option that suits you best, you'll want to decide how you want to manage the property. To assist with this decision-making process, this chapter will cover property management vs self-management. Throughout this chapter, we will present reasons why you might contemplate hiring a property manager and why you might choose to manage the property yourself.

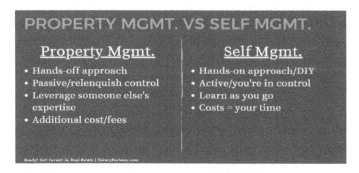

As an intro, let's review key points comparing property

management and self-management. When you have a property management company assist you with your property, it allows you to take a mostly hands-off approach to your property. This is because good property management companies have streamlined processes. They implement those processes to handle nearly everything related to renting your property on your behalf. It's beneficial for you as the property owner because it creates an opportunity for you to have passive involvement with your property's day-to-day activities. However, you must give up some level of decision-making to someone else. You will have to periodically check your property manager's work. For example, you must check your monthly statements to review the property's revenues and expenses. You also need to physically check your property from time to time to make sure things are working smoothly and your property is being well maintained through the property manager's efforts. However, for the most part, you will not need to be involved in operational activities like guest communication or coordinating property cleanings. By using a property manager, you leverage the expertise of professionals with extensive experience managing properties and tenants. To leverage the expertise of its employees, property management companies charge you fees for their services.

On the other hand, you have the option to self-manage your property. Self-managing a property is a very hands-on approach where you take full control and responsibility of your property's management activities. This approach can be highly active, giving you direct involvement and decision-making authority. Depending on your needs and objectives, this hands-on approach can be advantageous. With self-management, you'll learn as you go. This can present challenges initially because there will be aspects of property management that you are not familiar with. Over time, as you gain experience you will increase your knowledge and become more proficient at managing properties on your own. Although self-managing a property will not cost you additional money, it will cost you your time. You'll be responsible for tasks like marketing your property, managing bookings and leases, communicating with tenants, and property maintenance. Keep these factors in mind as you weigh the pros and cons of property management vs. self-management.

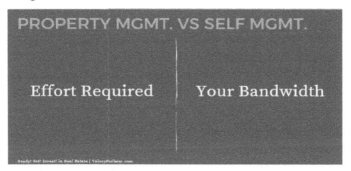

Continuing the comparison of property management and self-management, I'd like to share two factors that I always consider when deciding whether to hire a property manager or manage a property myself. These two factors are the level of effort required to manage a property and the amount of time and bandwidth I can dedicate to operating a property.

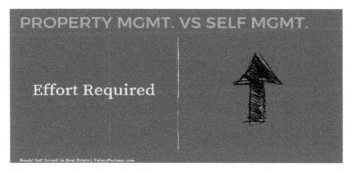

The level of effort required is a critical consideration when it comes to property management. I previously covered this in more detail, highlighting the differences between long-term and short-term rentals. For example, with a long-term rental that has a 12-month lease, your initial effort involves engaging with potential tenants to learn more about them, conducting background checks, preparing a lease for them to sign, and ensuring they are a suitable fit for your property. This initial effort can feel like a lot of leg work. However, once they are settled in, you might not hear from them for several months if everything goes smoothly. Therefore, long-term leases typically demand minimal ongoing effort from you, if you have done your due diligence on the front end and you keep the property well maintained.

On the opposite end of the spectrum, short-term rentals require significantly more effort to operate. You will frequently receive inquiries from potential guests checking for availability, asking questions about your property's location and policies, and needing guidance on the check-in and check-out processes. Additionally, you must manage the turnover process and coordinate cleaning the property after each guest. Given the frequent turnover of guests compared with a long-term rental, this effort can become a demanding, recurring task, especially if guests stay for only 2, 3, or 4 days at a time. As the effort and workload associated with managing a property increases, it often prompts me to consider employing property management services to assist.

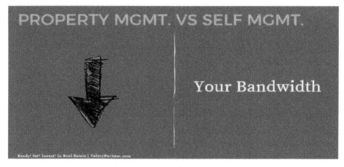

Your available bandwidth is another important factor to consider when deciding between property management and self-management. If you have a full-time job, children to take care of, or various commitments that demand a significant portion of your time, you might not be able to dedicate the necessary time and effort to manage a property effectively. If that is the case, handling a long-term rental might be more manageable for you due to its lower operational demands. On the other hand, properties with mid-term or short-term rental setup may become overwhelming if your schedule is already packed.

In general, as your bandwidth or available time goes down due to other responsibilities, it becomes more practical to hire a property management company to oversee your property. However, if you have tons of free time, prefer maintaining control over property management activities, and don't mind the fast turnover of shorter-term rentals, then self-management might be the way to go. Having more available bandwidth can create more options for you to manage your properties.

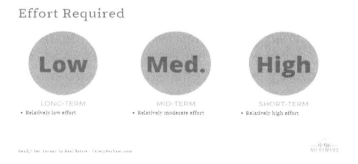

I covered effort required from a high level. Let's dive deeper based on the different rental durations.

Long-term rentals typically demand a relatively low level of effort once they are set up and running smoothly. Although there might be some initial work involved, such as screening tenants and preparing the property, provided you have a good tenant in place, you often won't need to invest much additional effort outside of maintenance related issues. Your rental can become even more convenient if your tenant decides to renew their lease for another term.

Mid-term rentals, as the name suggests, are rentals that have a duration somewhere in the middle of a short- and long-term rental. For example, mid-term rental lease durations could be one month, three months, or six months as previously noted. Mid-term rentals typically require more effort than long-term rentals but less than short-term ones. The comparatively moderate level of effort stems from mid-term rentals offering more amenities and convenience than long term rentals but turning over less frequently than short-term rentals.

Finally, short-term rentals, with frequent turnovers and inquiries, are the most demanding in terms of effort. They require more communication to answer questions from potential guests, more operational oversight to assist with processes like check-in and check-out, and property inspections, cleaning and maintenance between bookings. If you offer additional amenities or personalized touches to enhance the guest experience, such as toiletries or special gifts, expect an even higher level of effort.

In summary, long-term rentals tend to be the least demanding, followed by mid-term rentals, and short-term rentals are usually the most effort-intensive option.

Your Bandwidth

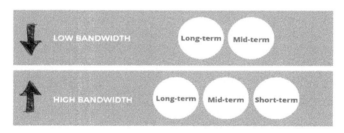

Use the simplified diagram above as a guide when considering which rental type you could self-manage based on your available bandwidth.

If you have low bandwidth, you might want to consider long-term or mid-term property rentals. If you have high bandwidth, the sky is pretty much the limit. If you genuinely enjoy the work involved in rental management and engaging with people, you might decide that you have available time to handle several long-term rental properties simultaneously or any combination of the rental types discussed. For those who have quite a bit of bandwidth but are new to managing property, a mid-term or possibly a short-term rental could be a good option.

Think about how much time you want to commit to rental management. Are you purchasing property because you want a more passive income stream? If that is the case, hiring a property manager who you pay to assist is likely the best option. In contrast, if you have ample bandwidth, enjoy interacting with people, and like being involved with rental operation activities, you could self-manage to grow your experience while avoiding property management fees.

Chapter 12 Activities

Review the chapter questions and enter the answers in the lesson's worksheet in the Ready! Set! Invest! In Real Estate Blueprint located at the end of this book.

- Based on your bandwidth, do you have the time to self-manage a property?

- Based on your previous answer as well as the effort required to manage each type of property, does this change your thoughts on whether to have a property manager assist you with a property vs managing a property yourself? Why or why not?

Chapter 13 Self-Managed Properties: How to better streamline self-managed properties

TODAY'S DISCUSSION

OUTLINE OF TOPICS

Self Managed Properties

How to better streamline self-managed properties

Ready: Set: Invest: In Real Estate · Valery-Parham.com

In the previous chapter, I highlighted key factors to consider when making the decision between employing a property management company or self-managing your property. In this chapter, I'll share some ideas for streamlining the property management process if you choose to manage the property yourself.

Making Self-management Easier

YOU'VE DECIDED THAT YOU MAY BE ABLE TO HANDLE MANAGING A PROPERTY YOURSELF AND YOU THINK YOU MIGHT EVEN ENJOY IT. NOW WHAT?

Ready: Set: Invest: In Real Estate · ValeryParham.com

After absorbing the content up to this point, some of you might have decided that you're up for the challenge of managing the property yourself to gain hands-on experience. For those of you who want to try self-management, I'll outline methods to make the DIY property management process easier.

LIST ON AIRBNB

1. SIMPLE TO USE
2. EASY, STEP-BY-STEP LISTING PROCESS
3. LOTS OF VISITORS AND TRAFFIC
4. SIMPLE TO COMPARE/RESEARCH
   COMPETITOR LISTINGS
5. CONFIGURABLE RENTAL OPTIONS
6. EASY CALENDAR MANAGEMENT
7. EASY INTEGRATED PAYMENT SYSTEM
8. EXPANDING TO INCLUDE BOTH
   SHORT-TERM AND MID-TERM
   CUSTOMER BASES

First, if you're thinking about a furnished rental, it's advisable to start on Airbnb. Why, you might ask? For starters, the Airbnb platform is extremely simple to use and has a lot of great functionality. It has an easy step-by-step listing process that continues to be improved over time. You'll receive prompts to add new pieces of information to your listing, making it more detailed and informative for potential guests. Having a detailed listing helps you to deliver more value to people who are on Airbnb browsing for properties. As previously discussed, Airbnb has substantial visitor traffic, making it a prime platform for listing your property.

On Airbnb, it's straightforward and convenient for you to review other people's listings and compare them to your own. This helps you research to gauge how your listing stacks up against others. Compared to similarly sized properties in your area, is your property competitively priced? Airbnb offers a wide range of configurable rental options, allowing you to customize your listing. This means you can decide whether to permit additional guests and charge extra for them, allow pets, or offer discounts and incentives to attract potential guests. It's super easy and simple to manage your property calendars on Airbnb. You can mark specific days as unavailable, for instance, when you're going on vacation and won't be available to manage the property. Additionally, if you're using other platforms for marketing and your property gets booked through them, you can block those dates on your Airbnb calendar to prevent double bookings. Airbnb also simplifies the process of collecting payments. Payment collection is handled directly through

Airbnb's platform. To receive your payout via direct deposit, all you have to do is link to your preferred bank account.

Another great thing about Airbnb is it is expanding to include both short-term and mid-term customer bases. Since the pandemic, remote work has become increasingly common. Airbnb is actively gathering information about the preferences of these types of customers. Airbnb's platform has adapted to also highlight longer-term stays in the search parameters. Airbnb is no longer solely associated with vacation rentals for a few days. It now also caters to the mid-term customer base as well. These are all reasons why I recommend getting started on Airbnb for furnished rentals.

LIST ON FURNISHED FINDER

1. GREAT MID-TERM/LONG-TERM,
   PROFESSIONAL NICHE
2. SIMPLE, LOW-COST SOLUTION
3. SIMPLE TO COMPARE/RESEARCH
   COMPETITOR LISTINGS
4. TRANSPARENT, LOW FEE OPTIONS FOR
   POTENTIAL RENTERS
5. SUPPLEMENT WITH OTHER SERVICES
   LIKE STATE SPECIFIC LEASES,
   KEYCHECK, AVAIL

After listing on Airbnb, you should also consider using a platform like Furnished Finder. I personally think Furnished Finder is a great choice, especially for mid-term rentals. This website and app cater to travel nurses and other professionals who are staying in a location for a few months. Sometimes users will even need space for up to 12 months or more. It's a great marketplace platform for mid-term rental use cases.

Furnished Finder is particularly appealing because it offers a low-cost solution. At the time of writing this, Furnished Finder only charges a very low annual fee to use the platform. Similar to Airbnb, Furnished Finder makes it very easy for you to compare your property to others in your area. You can easily research what other listings in your vicinity offer in terms of pricing, amenities, and other details by browsing existing listings.

Another fantastic thing about Furnished Finder, unlike Airbnb, is that it does not impose any additional fees on your potential renters. Airbnb, due to its extensive presence and business model, includes various fees on top of your monthly rental rate. However, with Furnished Finder, you can set prices and keep fees low, or even nonexistent, because the Furnished Finder platform won't charge any extra fees to you or your renters, aside from their annual service fee.

Furnished Finder's platform is not as robust or integrated as Airbnb's. However, it's fairly simple to supplement the services you need from other websites and apps. Let's review some additional tools and processes that can make managing your property easier if you choose to leverage Furnish Finder or other marketplace rental platforms.

SUPPLEMENTAL SERVICES

1. AUTOMATIC BILL PAY WITH MONTHLY REVIEW
2. STATE-SPECIFIC LEASE CREATION
3. BACKGROUND CHECKS THROUGH KEYCHECK
4. RENT COLLECTION AUTOMATION THROUGH AVAIL
5. RECURRING LAWNCARE SERVICES THROUGH GREEN PAL
6. RECURRING SERVICES (E.G. CLEANING SERVICES) THROUGH HANDY

KEYCHECK

avail

GREENPAL

handy

First, I strongly recommend automating your bill payments. Ensure that all expenses, such as the mortgage, utilities (if you're including them for a fully furnished rental), water bills, cable bills, and electric bills, are paid on time. Set up automatic payments for these bills, and periodically review them on a monthly basis to ensure everything aligns with your expectations. This is a critical step.

Next is lease creation. If you use a platform like Furnished Finder, they offer a service that can help you create state-specific leases. With Furnish Finder, you are in charge of managing the tenant relationship, so you need to establish a lease that outlines the terms of the rental relationship. Furnish

Finder gives you the ability to create state-specific leases. You can take the lease agreement, and have it reviewed by a lawyer for an additional layer of assurance that your lease complies with state and local laws. This also ensures that it is well-drafted, doesn't omit anything important, and doesn't contain any contradictions. Remember lawyers are an important resource on your Real Estate Dream Team. Do not hesitate to leverage these resources to seek legal advice when necessary.

Another tool to consider is Key Check. Key Check provides you with the means to conduct background checks on potential tenants. If someone is interested in renting your property, you will want to gain insights into their rental history. You can find out if they have a history of eviction, if they've consistently paid rent on time, or other pertinent information such as their current employment status. Key Check offers an inexpensive way to perform background checks efficiently.

Next, let's discuss rent collection. This is a crucial aspect of property management because it's how you generate income. I know you want to get paid as effortlessly as possible, so you'll want to automate this process. I recommend using Avail for this purpose. Avail offers a convenient solution for landlords. Not only can you create your property listing on Avail, but it also allows you to publish your listing on other popular rental sites like Realtor.com. Additionally, Avail provides you with a customizable rental application. The key advantage here is the streamlined rent collection process. Avail makes it incredibly easy for tenants to pay rent by providing clear instructions. Tenants receive reminders when payments are due, and they have the flexibility to pay using their checking account or a credit card. This user-friendly approach simplifies the rent payment process, making it hassle-free for both you and your tenants.

You'll also want to automate certain services to ensure the maintenance of your property. One crucial aspect, particularly for curb appeal, is lawn care. I've used services like GreenPal and Lawn Starter to set up recurring lawn care services. These service platforms allow you to find local service providers in your area. You can review their past work, obtain quotes, and select the right person for the job. These are nice options to help you manage your lawn care needs.

Other resources to consider are Handy, Task Rabbit, and Mendbnb. The Handy and Task Rabbit platforms can be used to find skilled professionals to address unexpected issues. Using these platforms, you can find individuals for various tasks, whether it's handyman services or cleaning. It's a convenient option when you need assistance in a hurry, and you can also set up recurring services. They are worth exploring for a wide range of property-related services. A similar maintenance-related service that I have enjoyed using is Mendbnb. With Mendbnb, you pay a low monthly fee. If an unexpected maintenance related item pops up, you simply create a service request, and the Mendbnb team will select an appropriate resource to address the issue. Mendbnb offers peace of mind because you know you have a team on standby if and when needed.

These are just a few examples of places where you can find supplemental services that will significantly streamline your processes if you choose to self-manage your property.

I love a good visual, so let's take a look at what it might look like to set up the process. I talked about the resources and processes earlier, but sometimes seeing a visual representation can be very helpful.

1. Set up automatic bill pay: This is crucial to ensure that all your bills, including mortgage, utilities, and more, are

paid on time. Your property is your asset setup to make money. To ensure that basic bills are paid on time automate this step and review payments monthly.

2. Create the listing: Whether it's on Airbnb, Furnished Finder, or another platform, setting up a detailed and attractive listing is essential for attracting renters. If you have unfurnished properties, platforms like Avail can help you list them on Realtor.com and other sites.

3. Leases and Screening: If you are using platforms where you have a more direct connection with potential renters (e.g. Furnished Finder), you will need a way to screen potential renters and create leases. These are two very critical steps that can make or break your self-management experience. Services like Key Check can assist with background checks. Avail offers various features, including rent collection and listing your properties on platforms like Realtor.com to expand their visibility.

4. Automate rent collection: Use services like Avail to streamline rent collection, providing easy payment options for your tenants, along with reminders for due dates. It can even charge late fees when necessary. If you use Airbnb, collecting payments will be a breeze. These platforms make it simple to collect rent payments and deposit them into your chosen bank account.

5. Schedule maintenance services: For lawn care and other property maintenance needs, platforms like GreenPal, Handy, and Mendbnb can help you set up recurring services or find professionals when necessary.

Now that you understand the overall picture, I thought it would be helpful to provide you with some examples of what it looks like when you're behind the scenes in Airbnb's platform.

With Airbnb, you get a high-level overview of important information pertaining to your rental property. You can see upcoming reservations, current guests, and any steps you can take to enhance your listing's visibility. It gives you quick access to all your messages and communications with current and potential guests. Airbnb's platform also reminds you if you haven't replied to messages within a certain timeframe. As mentioned previously, Airbnb has a handy calendar where you can manage and view everything in one place. Having convenient access to all this information helps you stay organized and responsive.

Airbnb also allows you to keep track of the number of listings you have. At the time of writing this book, I have three listings. Two of them are active and one is unlisted. In the case of the unlisted property, I have a month-to-month tenant who has been there for almost two years, even though initially, he planned to stay for only three to six months. Therefore, I decided to unlist the rental unit on Airbnb. However, I can easily relist it on Airbnb when he decides to move.

You can also access insights and statistics related to your property, such as your overall rating, the number of reviews, your response rate, the number of views in a specific period, and your earnings. The screenshot above illustrates my transaction history with the properties listed on Airbnb, including completed and upcoming payments. Having all this information in one place makes it effortless to manage every aspect of your rental property. It's incredibly user-friendly and convenient.

Behind the scenes: Furnished Finder

Alright, now let's contrast that with Furnished Finder. With Furnished Finder, you can easily access all your booking inquiries. As potential renters send inquiries about your listings, you'll find all their information requests directly on the website or in the app. You can also view the parson's details and access their email addresses and phone numbers, making it easy for you to reach out and respond.

Another fantastic feature of Furnished Finder is that even if someone doesn't contact you directly, if the details they've provided align with what you're looking for in a tenant,

Furnished Finder will display their information in the "Matched Leads" section. This feature can be quite handy for identifying potential renters who meet your criteria.

For instance, if a potential renter is searching for a one-bedroom unit within a certain price range, and you happen to have a one-bedroom unit available in that price range, Furnished Finder will display the person in the "Matched Leads" section. Even if the person hasn't reached out to you directly, you'll still have access to the person's information. As mentioned earlier, you can also review additional details to gather more information. This includes their desired move-in and move-out dates, their workplace location, and their occupation. Having this additional information at your fingertips can be quite useful when deciding whether to reach out to these potential leads.

Behind the scenes: Furnished Finder

With Furnished Finder, you can also view "Unmatched Leads." In this example above, an individual looking for accommodation has two criteria that don't align with the space I listed. In this particular case, it appears that this individual needs a two-bedroom space, while one of my listings is a studio. This discrepancy is highlighted in red, along with the note regarding traveling with pets. Although I absolutely love pets, my current property management policy does not permit them, except in cases involving service animals or similar exceptions. This is just a quick example illustrating how Furnished Finder operates and the valuable tenant lead information it offers.

Behind the scenes: Avail.co

Now, let's revisit the topic of supplementing Furnished Finder, particularly with Avail. Above, I'm sharing a couple of screenshots from Avail to illustrate the value it provides.

Firstly, you can see all your rent rolls in Avail, displaying the property and the rent amounts due. You can delve into further details, including what you've collected so far, any overdue or returned payments, and any issues related to those payments. As I noted earlier, Avail also sends out reminders. Here's an example of a reminder notifying a tenant that their payment is due tomorrow, prompting the tenant to submit the payment due promptly. On the flip side of the transaction, I received an alert as the landlord, notifying me that the tenant initiated the rent payment. This and other alerts keep me informed about the status of payments.

Behind the scenes: Avail.co

Above are more examples to illustrate Avail's notification system. In the first example, Avail is notifying the tenant that their payment is due today, emphasizing it's their last

132

opportunity to submit the payment before potential issues arise. In the next screenshot, it's clear that the payment is overdue. Avail informs me that the tenant hasn't paid yet, and the payment is now past due. Finally, in the last screenshot, you can see a reassuring green checkbox, which typically indicates good news. In this case, it signifies that the payment will be deposited into my checking account today, which is always welcome news for landlords.

I hope you found this chapter informative and helpful. I covered a lot of information, and I wanted to provide real-life examples of what you can expect to see in platforms like Airbnb and Furnished Finder if you choose to manage your property on your own. Consider this a starting point, and keep in mind that you can continually research and learn about new platforms that emerge on the market to help streamline your processes and tailor them to your preferences.

Chapter 13 Activities

Review the chapter questions and enter the answers in the lesson's worksheet in the Ready! Set! Invest! In Real Estate Blueprint located at the end of this book.

- Of the platforms and services mentioned in this lesson, which were you already familiar with and which were new to you?

- Research the platforms that were new to you to learn more about the services they provide as well as their fees. Which would you most likely use to help you with your property management operations if any?

- What additional tasks might you need to automate to make self-managing your property easier and smooth? Tasks can be from the lesson or other tasks you have thought of.

INVEST!

Armed with your investment game plan and your own investment dream team, you'll have the confidence to acquire your next investment and start making the passive income you've always dreamed of!

Section 6 Ready! Set! Invest!

Chapter 14 Putting it all together: Armed with all the info and tools, let's build and finalize your plan!

You made it to section six! Great job. Get ready because you're in the home stretch. In this chapter, I'll review information from the previous sections and lessons so we can start pulling everything together and finalizing your plan.

In section 1, chapter two, I asked you to start with "why." Now, I want you to take some time to revisit that "why" as we dive deeper into outlining your specific goals. These goals can ultimately contribute to your "why" and make it a reality if you achieve the goals you identify.

I know you're probably already familiar with SMART goals, but I want us to make your goals even smarter. I'll cover how to do that next.

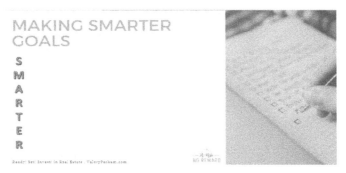

I want you to revisit the answer you provided in section 1, chapter 2. Read what you wrote for your "why" and start to write down a SMARTER goal that can get you one step closer to realizing your why.

For those of you who have heard of SMART goals or who have written SMART goals before, you are aware of what each of the first five letters stands for. "S" stands for specific, meaning your goal should be focused and outline a tangible outcome. If your goal isn't specific, you run the risk of having a goal that is too vague to achieve. Being specific helps you identify precisely what you want to achieve. "M" stands for measurable. When you have a way to measure your goal, you have a clear definition of what success in achieving your goal looks like. You'll also be able to measure your progress on your journey to achieving your goal.

After you have outlined how to measure your goal in terms of how much or how many, move on to the letter "A." "A" stands for achievable. This goal is meant to inspire motivation, and the only way it will be able to do that is if it is actually reasonable to achieve. It's okay to have a challenging goal, but make sure it's also something you truly believe you can achieve.

"R" stands for relevant. Making your goal relevant means making sure that it aligns very tightly with your why. If it aligns with your why, it means that what you are trying to achieve is a key top-of-mind priority for you. If your goal is not relevant to your why or you do not have a strong why to begin with this goal will remain on the back burner. Be truthful with yourself to make sure that you have started with a strong why, and this goal strongly supports your why.

Finally, "T" stands for time-bound. Every goal you set for

yourself should have a target completion date. This date should be a date that motivates you to really apply yourself and give your goal the focus and discipline necessary to achieve it in the timeframe that you have outlined. Setting a date answers when you plan to achieve your goal. Again, please be sure to make this date challenging yet realistic so you don't get discouraged along the way.

Following these key rules when setting goals creates a strong baseline for success, but we aren't going to stop there. We're going to make our goals smarter. To do this, we are going to add an "E" and an "R" to the SMART acronym.

MAKING SMARTER GOALS

S PECIFIC
M EASURABLE
A CHIEVABLE
R ELEVANT
T IME-BOUND
E MOTIONALLY CHARGING
R EWARDING

"E" stands for emotionally charged. This means that your goal should evoke a strong, positive, good feeling when you think about what it will feel like once you have achieved it. Making your goal measurable gives you a numeric metric to strive for, but making your goal evoke an emotion makes your goal exciting and its achievement meaningful.

The final letter, "R," stands for rewarding. This final letter is particularly important because it gives you an opportunity to outline what reward will make achieving this goal worth all of your time, energy, and sacrifice. When you are writing this component of the SMARTER goal, make sure you write down something that makes you feel great, accomplished, and rewarded. It can be something monetarily rewarding or something intrinsically rewarding. Just make sure the goal is something that will positively impact and improve your life.

Let's take a couple of minutes to walk through a few examples. For **specific**, consider: "I want to purchase a two-unit rental property in Nashville, Tennessee." That's pretty specific. With that example, you know what type of property you want to purchase (a duplex), and where you want to purchase that property (Nashville, TN).

For **measurable**, consider this example: "I want the duplex to generate positive cash flow of $1,000 to $2,000 per month." In this example, having a measurable goal of $1,000 to $2,000 helps you during the research phase. You'll use your goal metric to evaluate the different duplex opportunities available and determine if any can help you reach the desired goal.

Another example could be, "I want to save $10,000 for a down payment and buy my first duplex." In this example, the measurable part of your goal is being able to save $10,000 for your down payment.

For the achievable part of your SMARTER goal, you could set an objective like, "I can acquire a new property and start generating cash flow within the next six months. This is achievable because I have already established a savings plan and assembled the necessary team to make the property a reality." This approach ensures that your goal is attainable within the specified timeframe since you've already put the essential groundwork (e.g. type of property desired, down payment amount, dream team resources, etc.) in place.

"I have a family. Generating additional cash flow using an appreciating asset is crucial because I want to build wealth over time that will benefit me and my family." This is an example for **relevant**. It aligns with the overarching purpose of creating a financially strong legacy for yourself and your family. This has been a recurring theme throughout this program and is likely to resonate with many of you.

For the time-bound aspect of your SMARTER goal, you might state, "I want to acquire the new property within the next six months," as an example. It's important to consider all the necessary steps and requirements for purchasing the property and lay out a plan to ensure you can achieve this goal within the specified timeframe. When writing your SMARTER goals, always think about what's a reasonable and achievable timeframe for your specific property investment.

Next is **emotionally charged**. For this component of your SMARTER goal, consider this example: "My family is expanding soon because we're going to have our first baby! I want to spend as much time with the baby as possible, and having passive income would allow me to do that because the extra income will cover the additional expenses we will have." This description conveys the emotion and significance behind your goal, which is to provide for your growing family and spend quality time with your baby. When creating your SMARTER goals, aim to capture the emotions and positive feelings associated with achieving them. This will make your goals even more motivating and meaningful.

Lastly, we'll cover **rewarding**. A rewarding statement could be intrinsic as in the following example. "It would be very rewarding for me to teach my children how to build wealth in real estate and set them on the path to financial stability before they enter adulthood and the job market." This description highlights the personal fulfillment and satisfaction you would derive from imparting valuable financial knowledge and opportunities to your children, providing a strong incentive to achieve your goal.

Another example for rewarding could tie back to a monetary reward. Ponder this example: "Achieving the goal of owning a couple rental properties that generates $100,000 of passive income for me each year would allow me to replace my current income." For many people (including myself), replacing their full-time job income with a passive income source sounds incredibly appealing and motivating. This accomplishment is a highly rewarding endeavor, and one that I would be committed to achieving. Make sure that you select something that would be extremely rewarding to you personally.

Now you should understand the significance of making your goals not just smart but smarter. The addition of 'E' and 'R' ensures that your SMART goals are aligned with what matters most to you, increasing the likelihood of successfully achieving them. Remember, motivation comes from pursuing what truly matters to you, so keep that in mind as you craft your own SMARTER goals. When times get tough, your ability to see your goals to completion will depend on how much you care about the outcome (the "why") that is connected to your goals.

BEFORE INVESTING

READINESS CHECK

ARE YOU READY FOR PROPERTY
INVESTMENT?

Okay, now that we have covered how to set your goals, let's assess your plan so far and see if you are ready to invest.

Preparing to Invest

KNOW YOUR INVESTMENT READINESS.	CHOOSE YOUR INVESTMENT STRATEGY.
Module 2: Income, expenses, excess to spend, investment time frame, DTI Module 3: Dream Team	Module 4 Strategy examples: House hacking, house hop to hack, home rental additions, traditional Investment strategy (e.g. 20%+ downpayment)
IDENTIFY YOUR TARGET MARKET	DEFINE YOUR OPERATIONAL STRATEGY.
Module 5 Niche Opportunities: furnished vs unfurnished, long-, mid-, short-term, or non residential use rentals.	Module 6 Property Management vs self management

140

First, let's review your investment readiness. To do this, let's refer to section 1, chapter four, where you learned about budgeting and understanding where your money goes. By completing the income and budget spreadsheets, you should now have a clear understanding of your monthly income, expenses, and any surplus funds available for covering a new loan on an investment property. In the same chapter assignment, you also established a timeframe for when you plan to begin your investment journey. Subsequently, in section two, we explored the essential dream team resources to involve along your real estate journey. If you've successfully completed all the assignments from these lessons, you should possess a solid foundation for evaluating your investment readiness and next step.

In section three, the focus was on defining your investment strategy. I recommend revisiting section 3, chapter nine, to confirm your strategy choice and engage in discussions with a Realtor. If you have made it to this point, and you do not already have a Realtor who you are working with, I am happy to speak with you and assist (email: info@valeryparham.com, phone: 615-560-6400). Additionally, take a moment to review the various financing options and seek guidance from your preferred lender.

The chapters in section four assisted in outlining the options for identifying your target niche market. Consider whether you're preparing the property for short-term furnished rentals, catering to traditional long-term renters who don't require furnishings, or exploring non-residential uses such as creating spaces for photographers and content creators.

Section six covered management strategies to help you determine whether you want to enlist a property management company to handle day-to-day operations or manage the property yourself. If you've diligently completed the assignments up to this point, you should have established a solid foundation and a reasonable level of preparedness.

You've invested a significant amount of time and effort up to this point. Know that "Success occurs where opportunity meets preparation." Your level of preparedness positions you to seize any new opportunity that aligns with your goals.

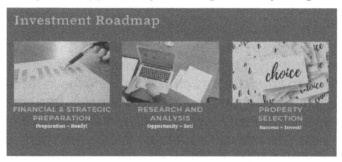

I like to interpret that quote in the following manner: financial and strategic preparation equals readiness. Once you are ready, you can delve into researching and analyzing current opportunities while positioning yourself for new opportunities that pop up. You are well-equipped to act swiftly on any opportunity that aligns with the criteria you've outlined in your SMARTER goal. Ultimately, being in control and in the driver's seat means you have a wide array of choices at your disposal, allowing you to invest in a property that contributes to your overall success, whatever that means for you.

Common Pitfalls

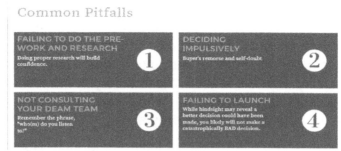

FAILING TO DO THE PRE-WORK AND RESEARCH Doing proper research will build confidence.	**1**	DECIDING IMPULSIVELY Buyer's remorse and self-doubt	**2**
NOT CONSULTING YOUR DREAM TEAM Remember the phrase, "who(m) do you listen to?"	**3**	FAILING TO LAUNCH While hindsight may reveal a better decision could have been made, you likely will not make a catastrophically BAD decision.	**4**

Before I continue, I want to pause and take a moment to address some common pitfalls that I hope you can avoid. Failing to do the pre-work and research is a crucial misstep. I understand that there has been a lot of content and assignments, but reading the content and doing the assignments is vital to ensure that you haven't missed anything. You want to approach this process from all angles and make sure you fill in any gaps in your knowledge to build a successful plan.

Next, research is essential. Now that you have your foundation, know what you're looking for, understand your financing options, know various rental strategies, and have your dream team in place, it's time to start looking at different opportunities. You'll likely work with your Realtor for this, but I'm emphasizing this because thorough research will elevate your confidence and help you identify the right investment property for you.

Deciding impulsively is another pitfall to avoid. Rushing into a decision without clear thinking and planning can lead to buyer's remorse and self-doubt. Preparedness, research, and comfort with your decisions will boost your confidence and make this journey smoother. I work with clients all the time who are just getting started on their real estate journeys. I will tell you the process can be emotionally taxing and make you feel as if you are on an emotional rollercoaster. Do yourself a favor and do the necessary pre-work and research. If you have a basic plan and are comfortable moving forward, it'll make the roller coaster a little less scary.

Another common mistake is failing to consult your dream

team. If you've brought professionals onto your dream team for their expertise and knowledge, make sure to consult them and leverage their insights. The internet is a valuable resource, but not everything on the internet is true or relevant to your situation or municipality. For this reason, make sure you are working with knowledgeable professionals who can provide specific guidance for your deals and interests.

Lastly, there's the issue of failing to launch. Sometimes, individuals become overwhelmed by the volume of information they are receiving coupled with uncertainty. These things lead to inaction and paralysis. Making decisions can feel daunting. However, I want to emphasize that making a decision, even if you later find a better opportunity, is a step in the right direction. Given what you knew at the time, you made the best choice. Don't fear decision-making, as you're unlikely to make a catastrophically bad decision. You're a capable and informed individual who has put in the work and assembled the right team. Leveraging your efforts and team of professionals will drive you toward success. Simply make sure that you're putting one foot in front of the other and taking action to reach your goals.

Now, let's talk about your next steps. First and foremost, maintain a reliable cash flow. It may seem obvious, but it's crucial: do not quit your job. Your job is essential right now for various reasons. It helps you financially qualify for any loans you may need, and it provides stability to manage your current responsibilities along with the new ones that come with owning a property. Keep this in mind as a top priority—do not quit your job.

Secondly, define your SMARTER goals. This will be part of the assignment for this chapter. Go back to the section on SMARTER goals, reflect on the suggestions I provided regarding SMARTER goals, and begin outlining each component of the SMARTER Goals acronym as it pertains to your unique situation and specific goals.

Lastly, engage in thorough research. I've emphasized that it should not become paralyzing. You could potentially research endlessly and still not cover every possible scenario. Do as much research as you can comfortably handle and then transition into decision-making mode. Remember the saying, "over-analysis leads to paralysis," and we want to avoid anything that hinders your progress. Conduct comprehensive research but ensure that you continue to move forward in the process.

Chapter 14 Activities

Review the chapter questions and enter the answers in the lesson's worksheet in the Ready! Set! Invest! In Real Estate Blueprint located at the end of this book.

- Review your answers to the questions in the assignments in modules 2, 3, 4, 5, and 6. Make revisions as needed based on new information you have received.

- Outline SMARTER goals for your real estate investment(s) using the acronym S-M-A-R-T-E-R.

Chapter 15 Research Tips: Simple Tips for Initial Research

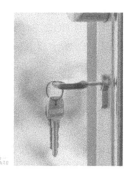

In the previous chapter, I mentioned that you should start conducting additional research as a next step. In this chapter, I want to briefly cover some simple tips and tricks for the initial research you'll need to do.

If you have created your Blueprint and completed actions to identify your real estate dream team, understand where your money is going, etc., you are likely ready to start researching potential properties. Where should you start your search? Let's look at a few options.

1. Start with the multiple listing service that covers your specific area. For example, here in Tennessee, we use Realtracs (www.realtracs.com). If you're in Tennessee, go to Realtracs and see what you can find. It also covers some areas in Alabama, Georgia, and Kentucky. If

you're in any of those states, feel free to check out Realtracs as well.

2. Another website that I use quite often is Realtor.com. Realtor.com is heavily used in the United States and has a ton of monthly active users, so it's definitely another place you can check out for your searches.

3. There are other websites as well that you may want to browse. Add Zillow, Trulia, and Homes.com to your list. Also check out LoopNet for commercial properties. Each of these sites has a search feature where you can enter your desired location and search for properties in that area.

You can also narrow down your search criteria if you're looking for something specific. For instance, you may want a residential property with a specific number of bedrooms and bathrooms, or you might be interested in multi-family properties like duplexes, triplexes, and quadplexes. You can set these parameters and many others in your search to ensure that only properties meeting your specified criteria show up in the results.

While the list of sites above is not an exhaustive list, it is a good place to start your searches. Once you've found properties that you like, it's a good idea to discuss them with your Realtor to confirm their availability. Sharing the properties you're interested in will help your Realtor understand your preferences and find a property that aligns with your wants and needs. With your search criteria and examples in hand, your Realtor will have ample information to locate a property that fits your goals.

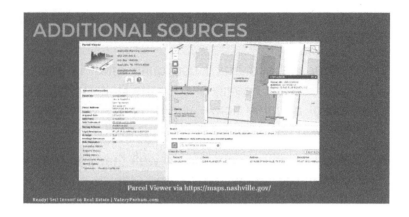

For more detailed information about a specific property you're interested in, you can explore maps.nashville.gov. This site has a parcel viewer feature. This tool allows you to access information about a particular property, including its ownership history and zoning history.

In areas with extensive property regulations, like Nashville, it's crucial to understand a property's zoning, as it may have specific requirements or restrictions. For example, certain zoning regulations may apply if you plan to operate short-term rental properties. Familiarizing yourself with the zoning types in your municipality can help you navigate these regulations.

If you find this level of research overwhelming, don't worry. Your Realtor can assist you with conducting additional research. This tool is provided as an example for those who wish to conduct some due diligence independently. If you don't live in Nashville, you may find a similar tool available in your area. Conduct a search or consult your Realtor for guidance.

As you continue to build your real estate portfolio, you may find it useful to research additional information about properties. For practice, you can visit maps.nashville.gov (or a similar site in your area) and enter a property address. If you already own a primary residence, you can enter its address to review the information available.

Another resource I find useful for quickly estimating monthly mortgage payments is Homes.com. While it may not provide the most precise figures, it can offer a ballpark estimate for different properties. Keep in mind that during the lending process, your lender will provide the most accurate information regarding your monthly payment for a specific loan amount.

In the first image, you can see a property and it's list price of $575,000. As you scroll down the page of the Homes.com website, there's a section that has a mortgage payment calculator. Based on the list price of $575,000 and an interest rate of 7.19%, here are 3 estimated payment examples:

- For a home priced at $575,000 with a 20% down payment (equivalent to $115,000) and other parameters held constant, the estimated monthly payment would be around $3,555.

- If you put down only 5%, which is $28,750, while keeping other parameters the same, your estimated monthly payment would be approximately $4,538.

What makes Homes.com particularly useful is its flexibility. You can adjust not only the down payment and interest rate but also the annual mortgage insurance. Other mortgage payment calculators do not let you manipulate this parameter. This feature of Homes.com is especially beneficial for those exploring zero to low down payment options that do not incur mortgage insurance costs. In such cases, Homes.com allows you to customize both the down payment and mortgage insurance components, providing you with a more accurate estimate of your monthly payment.

A question that often arises is how to estimate operating expenses for a new rental. Earlier I covered to illustrate methods for calculating cash flow and cap rate. Let's revisit that example and consider what monthly costs might be required to operate the property as a rental. As someone with experience, I have a good understanding of what to include in this category. However, as a general guideline, especially for those who already own a primary residence, you can think about the expenses you currently incur and estimate how much they cost you. If you're considering a property of a similar type or size, you may be able to estimate these costs based on what you already pay.

If you are currently renting, you can still apply a similar approach to estimate costs. For instance, if you're responsible for paying for electricity, water, or other utilities in your rental, or if you have separate bills for TV channels and internet, you can use these figures as estimates to gauge your potential expenses as a property owner. Keep in mind that this is an area where you may also benefit from consulting with other experts or seeking feedback to help you refine your estimates for operating expenses. The specific operating expenses you need to consider can vary depending on who covers these costs and whether you are pursuing a longer-term rental strategy or a shorter-term rental strategy.

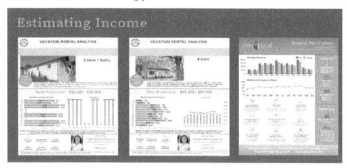

Next, let's discuss estimating your rental income. The approach you take and the income you generate will vary depending on your specific strategy. To illustrate this, I'll briefly explain how property management companies can provide proforma information to give you an idea of potential rental income.

In the first example, I received a proforma from a company for a duplex that I rent out. Each of the duplex's two units has two bedrooms and one bathroom. Their rental income projection ranges between $20,000 and $30,000. It's important to note that this particular duplex is primarily marketed to travel nurses and other professionals who require accommodations for time periods ranging from three to six months. The company estimated the income they could generate on each side of the duplex considering a mid-term rental strategy.

In the next example, the same company projected rental income for a different property, estimating it to be between $65,000 and $80,000. This property is a four-bedroom, three-bathroom home intended for short-term rentals, like Airbnb-style accommodations, attracting vacationers and short-stay guests.

I also contacted another company to get their estimate for the same four-bedroom, three-bathroom property. Their estimate is an average of $82,774, with the top-end projection being $96,514. These examples demonstrate the variation in rental income estimates, depending on factors such as property type, location, and rental strategy.

Let's look at some other considerations. The property management companies I contacted also provided supplementary information such as average occupancy rates, daily rates, and rental seasonality variations. These insights into expected income ranges for different seasons can be particularly valuable for those considering short-term rentals. If you plan to use property management services, don't hesitate to contact these companies to obtain estimates. Similarly, if you're interested in long-term rentals, you can reach out to long-term property management companies for income projections. This information serves as a starting point for your rental income estimates.

Another approach to gaining a deeper understanding of rental property income potential in your area is to use Realtor.com. This platform offers extensive information on rental properties. To access this information, simply navigate to the "rent" section on Realtor.com and enter your location of interest. You can also use the map view feature to narrow down your search to a specific area you're considering for your rental property. By zooming in on the map, you can identify properties similar to the type you're interested in, whether it's a two-bedroom, one-bath, three-bedroom, and so on. Explore these similar properties and note their rental rates in the target area you're researching. This hands-on approach can provide you with valuable insights into local rental property pricing trends.

If you're considering short-term rentals, you can follow a

similar approach on Airbnb. Use Airbnb's platform to explore listings in your target area. Use the map feature to narrow down your search to a specific location you're interested in. Examine listings that are similar to the type of property you plan to rent out. This allows you to review how these listings are presented, what features and amenities they highlight, and how they target their audience. For instance, if they cater to business professionals who require high-speed internet, this information can guide your property setup and listing presentation if you want to rent to that same target audience. There are numerous websites where you can conduct similar research, Realtor.com and Airbnb, are excellent starting points for your due diligence.

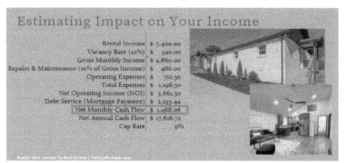

Another important step is to consider how a new rental could impact you in the short term. Consider the numbers from the duplex example covered earlier. Specifically, focus on the monthly cash flow. Use your income projections and expert advice to conduct a financial analysis. Understand what the bottom line means for you and then incorporate this information into the budgeting tool I introduced earlier in the program. This will help you see how the rental income and expenses fit into your overall financial picture. Once you start earning rental income, you can update the numbers in the budgeting tool to give you a more actuate picture of how the property's performance impacts your financials.

I also want to stress that it is crucial to build a financial cushion and have reserve funds in place. In the beginning there are unknown costs that will pop up. You need money to cover any unexpected costs to set up your rental for success. This is especially true when dealing with short- and mid-term rentals.

These rental property types will also likely need time before they can produce the projections provided by property management companies because bookings are heavily dependent on reviews which you won't have when you start.

We've covered short-term impact. Now let's discuss the long-term impact. You should also consider how property values are trending over time in your area. This aspect won't have an immediate effect like cash flow, but it will come into play later when you decide to sell the property or if you decide to take out equity in the future. It's essential to evaluate how real estate values are changing in your chosen location to make informed decisions about your investment's potential appreciation.

Your property's potential to increase in value is an extremely important factor to consider when thinking about your overall net worth. People who leverage their house as an asset by having renters pay for it get the benefit of generating money now and more money later when they sell. Having access to rental income now can satisfy a need for instant gratification. If that income is re-invested in the home to gradually pay down the mortgage while the house also increases in value, you'll see your net worth grow!

Chapter 15 Activities

Review the chapter questions and enter the answers in the lesson's worksheet in the Ready! Set! Invest! In Real Estate Blueprint.

- Of the research tools and options presented in this lesson, which do you think you will find the most helpful? Why?

- What additional research do you need to do to feel confident about your plan to make an investment in real estate? Which dream team resource(s) can assist?

- At this point, do you feel like you are ready to invest? Why or why not?

Chapter 16 Wrap Up

Thank you & good luck on your real estate journey!

Congratulations, and thank you immensely for your active participation! Best of luck on your real estate journey. I'm confident that many wonderful opportunities lie ahead for you, and I hope that reading this book has served as a valuable steppingstone in your journey.

Once more, I want to extend my congratulations. You've done it! You've reached this point after dedicating countless hours to reading the content in this book and absorbing the information. You've diligently completed all the chapter assignments and invested a great deal of thought and energy into crafting your own Blueprint. You should take immense pride in your accomplishments. You are now one step closer to acquiring your first or next property. I'm incredibly grateful that you've allowed me to be a part of this journey with you. Thank you once again!

As you take your next steps, I want to let you know that I am here to support you on your real estate investing journey. First, let's connect so I can learn more about you and real estate aspirations. Schedule a consultation meeting so we can have an initial discussion about your goals and your why. From there, we can have a deeper discussion about how I may be able to assist you with your next steps.

You might be wondering how to get in touch with me. If you're ready to schedule a meeting, please use my Calendly link. If, for any reason, that doesn't work for you, feel free to send me an email at Info@ValeryParham.com. Alternatively, you can reach me by phone or text at 615-560-6400. Stay connected and share your next steps with me, along with any significant takeaways and accomplishments, no matter how big or small. I love hearing from Wealth Creators like you! Now, go out there and turn your investment dreams into reality. **Ready! Set! Invest!**

Ready Set Invest Blueprint

Ready! Set! Invest!

In Real Estate Product Disclaimer

The information provided in this guide is provided on an "as is" and "as available" basis. Thus, all purchasers and/or readers of any expressly agree that their use or interpretation is done so at their sole and exclusive risk. It is provided only to promote basic real estate rental property investment education and inspiration. It is not intended as financial or investment advice and should not be used as the sole input for investments and investment decisions.

Neither Valery Parham nor their affiliates, licensors, suppliers or distributors will be held liable for indirect, incidental, special, consequential, or exemplary damages resulting from the use of the information or services provided.

The information and materials provided in this book and course come from a variety of sources, including the professional experiences of Valery Parham. Accordingly, the information in this program is copyright, 2023 © Ready! Set! Invest! In Real Estate and no part of it may in any form by electronic, mechanical, photocopying, recording, or any other means be reproduced, stored in a retrieval system or be broadcast, sold or transmitted without the prior permission of the author.

My Wealth Building Blueprint

A guide to profitable properties

Hey! I'm Valery, and I'm so happy you are reading this - because it means you're going to improve your overall financial health and start an incredible transformational journey. By completing this blueprint guide to create your own plan using the activities in my Ready! Set! Invest! in Real Estate Program, you'll learn how to achieve wealth, financial independence, and the freedom to spend your time the way you want through creating passive income sources from your real estate investments.

Throughout this book, I included my top tips and guidelines for how to grow your knowledge of real estate investing as part of a long-term wealth building lifestyle change. Starting and growing your real estate investment portfolio will give you more opportunities to increase your wealth to create a financial stability and independence for you, your family, and the generations that follow.

I've also included additional resources and tools to help you continue your success beyond this book.

About this Blueprint...

Here are some general guidelines to get the most from this guide:

- Review the chapters in sequential order, and do not skip any of the chapters.

- Complete your chapter assignments in sequential order. Do not skip any of the chapter assignments and answer each question in each chapter.

- After you read each chapter, answer the questions for each chapter in this Ready! Set! Invest! in Real Estate Blueprint guide.

- Some of the work you do for your assignments will be done in the Ready! Set! Invest! in Real Estate Blueprint Excel spread sheet. Save a digital copy of your filled out spreadsheet or print your answers and include in the corresponding section of this Ready! Set! Invest! in Real Estate Blueprint guide.

- If you have any questions about lesson content, lesson assignments, or other items, please do not hesitate to ask your questions. You may also submit questions to **info@valeryparham.com.**

- This Blueprint guide is broken into 3 sections: Ready! (Sections 1-2), Set! (Sections 3-5) and Invest! (Section 6). Complete all the assignments in each section to create your personalized plan.

- Have fun while you learn! Remember this program was setup to be all about YOU! Please do not feel intimidated by the content or the chapter assignments. If you need help, please ask. You may also connect with others in our Ready! Set! Invest! in Real Estate Wealth Creators accountability group to get ideas and suggestions as we go through the program. This is your opportunity to network with other like-minded people so make those connections!

LET'S GET STARTED!

Ready! Chapter Assignment Worksheets

Use subsequent pages to complete your Section 1-2, Chapter 1-7 Assignments.

Review the chapter and enter the answers to the questions below on the following page of the Ready! Set! Invest! in Real Estate Blueprint.
1. Do you currently rent or own?
2. Of the benefits outlined during this chapter, which ownership benefits appeal to you most?
3. Why are you most interested in those benefits?

Consider Real Estate

Provide your answers below.

The Benefits of Rental Property

PASSIVE INCOME SOURCE

#1

Rental property is a great way to create passive income. Passive income includes regular earnings from a source other than an employer or contractor. The Internal Revenue Service (IRS) says passive income can come from two sources: rental property or a business in which one does not actively participate, such as being paid book royalties or stock dividends.
~www.BankRate.com

FLEXIBILITY TO SELL

#2

People who own property have the flexibility to hold and rent their property or they can sell. Most people think of owning property as a very long-term commitment but buying a property with a mortgage doesn't have to be a 15-, 20- or 30-year commitment. When market conditions are favorable, the property can be sold, and if market conditions aren't favorable, the property can be rented until the market bounces back. This flexibility is a great benefit of rental property.

PROPERTY VALUE APPRECIATION

#3

Property ownership provides the owner an opportunity to make additional income from the sale of the property if the property's value increases. This increase in the property's value is called appreciation. There are many factors that play a part in property values, so a property's value is not guaranteed to increase, however, property values do generally tend increase over time.

SOMEONE ELSE PAYS

Owners of rental properties use other people's money (OPM) to pay for their assets. They do this by collecting rent. By using other people's paychecks (OPP), property owners can pay down the mortgage on the property (if they have a mortgage) while also taking advantage of appreciation with the goal to spend as little of their own money as possible. Creating a vehicle to use OPM and OPP to pay for own's assets is a phenomenal benefit of owning rental property.

#4

#5

INVESTMENT DIVERSIFICATION

Owning property is another way to diversify your investment portfolio, and it can provide an added layer of protection against risks. It's usually never good to put all your eggs in one basket so many investors use real estate to broaden their investment portfolios.

#6

TAX BENEFITS

The Internal Revenue Service allows you to deduct many expenses connected with rental property in the categories of:
• Ordinary and necessary expenses
• Improvements
• Depreciation
This means that you can deduct your insurance, interest on your mortgage, maintenance costs, and physical wear-and-tear on your property
~https://www.investopedia.com/

1. Print the No Risk No Reward Goal Achievement Affirmations list and place it somewhere where you will see it each day. Read these affirmations silently or out loud each day to encourage you throughout your real estate goal achievement journey.

2. Spend at least 30 focused minutes in a quiet space to write down your Why in the Ready! Set! Invest! in Real Estate Blueprint.

No Risk No Reward
Goal Achievement Affirmations

1. I can achieve anything with the right mindset, willpower, and desire.
2. I will only focus on goals that are aligned with my purpose.
3. I will set clear, focused goals, and I will work on 1 goal at a time, 1 day at a time.
4. I will take action mindfully so that I am prioritizing actions that move me toward completing my goals.
5. Failure is okay as long as I am unwilling to accept defeat.
6. If I fail, I am not a failure.
7. I will learn through failure, and I will try again and again until I achieve my goal.
8. I know failure is temporary because I chose to move past failures quickly.
9. I will start, and I will continue to make incremental progress forward.
10. I CAN and I WILL!

Building Your Foundation: Your WHY

Provide your answers below.

Review the chapter and enter the answers to the questions below on the following page of the Ready! Set! Invest! in Real Estate Blueprint.

1. Consider what you read in this chapter about Sylvia. What were some interesting takeaways you learned? Note: It could be one of the 5 noted in the chapter or other takeaways that resonated with you.

2. What are some creative ways Sylvia is leveraging her real estate? Are there any you would consider for your real estate journey?

3. Write down tax benefits you would receive or have received as a property owner and note additional tax benefits you would receive as a rental property owner.

Section 1 | Chapter 3 Worksheet

Creative Inspiration

Provide your answers below.

Section 1 | Chapter 4 Activities

Review the chapter and enter the answers to the questions below in the Ready! Set! Invest! in Real Estate Blueprint Excel spread sheet.

1. Know Where Your Money Goes - Fill out the income & budget spreadsheets provided in your bonus materials.

2. Understand Your Net Worth - Fill out the Net Worth and Target Net Worth spreadsheets provided in your bonus materials. Note: If your net worth is negative, zero, or off target, try not to be intimidated, frustrated, or feel down. We will revisit net worth in Section 7. Remember, the goal at this point is to understand your starting point and where you are now.

3. Start Somewhere Then Grow - List your current starting point. Where would you like to start (primary residence or investment property)? When is your goal to invest (e.g. ASAP, 1-3 months, 3-6 months, 6-12 months, more than 12 months)?

Section 1 | Chapter 4 Worksheet

Start Somewhere Then Grow - When is your goal to invest (e.g. ASAP, 1-3 months, 3-6 months, 6-12 months, more than 12 months)? Provide your answers below.

Section 2 | Chapter 5 Activities

Review the chapter and enter the answers to the questions below on the following page of the Ready! Set! Invest! in Real Estate Blueprint.

1. Reflect on the information provided in this lesson. Based on your specific needs, why do you think you need a realtor on your real estate dream team?

2. Are you currently working with a realtor? If not, find one this week, add the Realtor's name and contact information to your Blueprint, and contact him or her to make an introduction. Note: I'm happy to work with you or provide a recommendation. Email **info@valeryparham.com** if you need assistance with selecting a realtor.

3. Based on your specific needs, why do you think you need a lender on your real estate dream team?

4. Are you currently working with a lender? If not, find one this week, add the lender's name and contact information to your Blueprint, and contact him or her to make an introduction.

Why you need a Realtor on the Dream Team

WHAT TO KNOW

7 Reasons to Work With a REALTOR®

REALTORS® aren't just agents. They're professional members of the National Association of REALTORS® and subscribe to its strict code of ethics. This is the REALTOR® difference for home buyers:

1. **Ethical treatment.**
   Every REALTOR® must adhere to a strict code of ethics, which is based on professionalism and protection of the public. As a REALTOR®'s client, you can expect honest and ethical treatment in all transaction-related matters. The first obligation is to you, the client.

2. **An expert guide.**
   Buying a home usually requires dozens of forms, reports, disclosures, and other technical documents. A knowledgeable expert will help you prepare the best deal, and avoid delays or costly mistakes. Also, there's a lot of jargon involved, so you want to work with a professional who can speak the language.

3. **Objective information and opinions.**
   REALTORS® can provide local information on utilities, zoning, schools, and more. They also have objective information about each property. REALTORs® can use that data to help you determine if the property has what you need. By understanding both your needs and search area, they can also point out neighborhoods you don't know much about but that might suit your needs better than you'd thought.

4. **Expanded search power.**
   Sometimes properties are available but not actively advertised. A REALTOR® can help you find opportunities not listed on home search sites and can help you avoid out-of-date listings that might be showing up as available online but are no longer on the market.

5. **Negotiation knowledge.**
   There are many factors up for discussion in a deal. A REALTOR® will look at every angle from your perspective, including crafting a purchase agreement that allows enough time for you to complete inspections and investigations of the property before you are bound to complete the purchase.

6. **Up-to-date experience.**
   Most people buy only a few homes in their lifetime, usually with quite a few years in between each purchase. Even if you've done it before, laws and regulations change. REALTORS® handle hundreds of transactions over the course of their career.

7. **Your rock during emotional moments.**
   A home is so much more than four walls and a roof. And for most people, property represents the biggest purchase they'll ever make. Having a concerned, but objective, third party helps you stay focused on the issues most important to you.

Source: Realtor Magazine

REALTOR® Magazine | RealtorMag.Realtor.org
Copyright 2015. All rights reserved.

NATIONAL ASSOCIATION of REALTORS®

Section 2 | Chapter 5 Worksheet

Realtors & Lenders

Provide your answers below.

Section 2 | Chapter 5 Worksheet

Realtors & Lenders

Provide your answers below.
(additional space for your answer if needed)

Review the chapter and enter the answers to the questions below on the following page of the Ready! Set! Invest! in Real Estate Blueprint.

1. Based on the information provided, what property management benefits are the most important to you?
2. Research 3 local property management companies and contact each to learn about their rates and what is included in their rates.
3. Review the websites of each of the large property management companies discussed in this chapter then compare the large property management companies with the local property management companies. Which companies appeal to you the most? Why?

Section 2 | Chapter 6 Worksheet

Property Management

Provide your answers below.

Property Management

Provide your answers below.
(additional space for your answer if needed)

Review the chapter and enter the answers to the questions below on the following page of the Ready! Set! Invest! in Real Estate Blueprint.

1. Based on the information provided, what additional resources do you think you will need on your real estate dream team?
2. Research service providers for each of your needs. Remember to check out the resources listed in the Ready! Set! Invest! in Real Estate Resource Guide as well. Which companies/providers are you considering?
3. Contact each service provider to learn about their rates and what is included in their rates.
4. List the names and contact information of the service providers who you would like to add to your real estate dream team.

Section 2 | Chapter 7 Worksheet

More Dream Team Resources

Provide your answers below.

Section 2 | Chapter 7 Worksheet

More Dream Team Resources

Provide your answers below.
(additional space for your answer if needed)

Set! Chapter Assignment Worksheets

Use subsequent pages to complete your Section 3-5, Chapter 8-13 Assignments.

Section 3 | Chapter 8 Activities

Review the chapter and enter the answers to the questions below on the following page of the Ready! Set! Invest! in Real Estate Blueprint.

1. Review NOI and capitalization rate. Did you know about these financial metrics? Did you know how to calculate them? Do you still have questions? If so, what questions do you have?
2. Prior to this chapter, had you considered being able to live for free or virtually free or generating a positive cash flow from your real estate investments? How would living free or virtually free change your life? How would generating a positive cash flow change your life?
3. Had you previously considered what to do if you have a vacancy for an extended period of time? Which option(s) presented resonated with you most? What other options can you think of?

Section 3 | Chapter 8 Worksheet

Financial Considerations
Provide your answers below.

Section 3 | Chapter 8 Worksheet

Financial Considerations

Provide your answers below.
(additional space for your answer if needed)

Section 3 | Chapter 9 Activities

Review the chapter and enter the answers to the questions below on the following page of the Ready! Set! Invest! in Real Estate Blueprint.

1. Of the rental property investment options presented in this chapter, which seems like the route you would most likely take? If you have another route you have been considering, please list that option in your answer.
2. Of the financing options discussed, which seem like some options you would like to consider for your entry into your investment property? What questions do you have about these options?

Section 3 | Chapter 9 Worksheet

Creative Options
Provide your answers below.

Section 3 | Chapter 9 Worksheet

Creative Options

Provide your answers below.
(additional space for your answer if needed)

Section 4 | Chapter 10 Activities

Review the chapter and enter the answers to the questions below on the following page of the Ready! Set! Invest! in Real Estate Blueprint.

1. Based on the information presented in this chapter, which rental setup and duration appeals to you most as starting point for your property rental?

2. Are you considering using marketplace sites like Airbnb or Furnished Finder? If so, which marketplaces appeal to you most? Which are you least interested in?
3. Are you interested in other property rental websites that were not covered in this chapter? If so, please list those websites, and describe why you are interested in them.

Section 4 | Chapter 10 Worksheet

Know Your Niche

Provide your answers below.

Section 4 | Chapter 10 Worksheet

Know Your Niche

Provide your answers below.
(additional space for your answer if needed)

Review the chapter and enter the answers to the questions below on the following page of the Ready! Set! Invest! in Real Estate Blueprint.

1. Prior to reading this chapter, were you familiar with non-residential use location rentals?
2. After reading this chapter, would you consider this use for your rental property or are you more interested in traditional residential rental property uses?
3. If you are interested in non-residential use location rentals, what type interests you most? e.g. meetings, events, production?

Section 4 | Chapter 11 Worksheet

Additional Niche Options

Provide your answers below.

Section 4 | Chapter 11 Worksheet

Additional Niche Options

Provide your answers below.
(additional space for your answer if needed)

Review the chapter and enter the answers to the questions below on the following page of the Ready! Set! Invest! in Real Estate Blueprint.

1. Based on your bandwidth, do you have the time to self-manage a property?

2. Based on your previous answer as well as the effort required to manage each type of property, does this change your thoughts on whether to have a property manager assist you with a property vs managing a property yourself? Why or why not?

Section 5 | Chapter 12 Worksheet

Property Management vs. Self-Management

Provide your answers below.

Property Management vs. Self-Management

Provide your answers below.
(additional space for your answer if needed)

Review the chapter and enter the answers to the questions below on the following page of the Ready! Set! Invest! in Real Estate Blueprint.

1. Of the platforms and services mentioned in this lesson, which were you already familiar with and which were new to you?

2. Research the platforms that were new to you to learn more about the services they provide as well as their fees. Which would you most likely use to help you with your property management operations if any?

3. What additional tasks might you need to automate to make self-managing your property easier and smooth? Tasks can be from the lesson or other tasks you have thought of.

Self-Managed Properties

Provide your answers below.

Section 5 | Chapter 13 Worksheet

Self-Managed Properties

Provide your answers below.
(additional space for your answer if needed)

Invest! Chapter Assignment Worksheets

Use subsequent pages to complete your Section 6, Chapter 14-16 Assignments.

Review the chapter and enter the answers to the questions below on the following page of the Ready! Set! Invest! in Real Estate Blueprint.

1. Review your answers to the questions in the assignments in modules 2, 3, 4, 5, and 6. Make revisions as needed based on new information you have received.

2. Outline SMARTER goals for your real estate investment(s) using the acronym S-M-A-R-T-E-R.

Pulling It All Together

Provide your answers below.

Pulling It All Together

Provide your answers below.
(additional space for your answer if needed)

Section 6 | Chapter 15 Activities

Review the chapter and enter the answers to the questions below on the following page of the Ready! Set! Invest! in Real Estate Blueprint.

1. Of the research tools and options presented in this lesson, which do you think you will find the most helpful? Why?

2. What additional research do you need to do to feel confident about your plan to make an investment in real estate? Which dream team resource(s) can assist?

3. At this point, do you feel like you are ready to invest? Why or why not?

Section 6 | Chapter 15 Worksheet

Research Tips

Provide your answers below.

Section 6 | Chapter 15 Worksheet

Research Tips

Provide your answers below.
(additional space for your answer if needed)

Section 6 | Chapter 16 Activities

Review the chapter and enter the answers to the questions below on the following page of the Ready! Set! Invest! in Real Estate Blueprint.

1. How can you get in touch with me if you need help or have questions?

2. How can you access bonus materials, supplemental videos, and more?

3. Write down your next steps, significant takeaways, and accomplishments and share those items with me. I can't wait to hear from you.

Section 6 | Chapter 16 Worksheet

Wrap Up

Provide your answers below.

Section 6 | Chapter 16 Worksheet

Wrap Up

Provide your answers below.
(additional space for your answer if needed)

Thanks!

Thank you for reading and completing this guide! I hope you found it interesting, and I hope it helps you achieve your goals!

Wishing you all the best and much success,

Valery Parham

Milton Keynes UK
Ingram Content Group UK Ltd.
UKHW022049040124
435404UK00016B/466